girdles
and other harnesses
I have known

Joyce Harries
illustrated by Shelley Wales

Rita —
more stories
please —
Joyce Harries

Lone Pine Publishing

girdles and other harnesses I have known

© 2000 by Joyce Harries and Lone Pine Publishing
First printed in 2000   10 9 8 7 6 5 4 3 2 1
Printed in Canada

The Publisher: Lone Pine Publishing

10145-81 Ave.	202A, 1110 Seymour St.	1901 Raymond Ave. SW, Suite C
Edmonton, AB T6E 1W9	Vancouver, BC V6B 3N3	Renton, WA 98055
Canada	Canada	USA

Website: http://www.lonepinepublishing.com

Canadian Cataloguing in Publication Data

Harries, Joyce, 1928–
   Girdles and other harnesses I have known

   ISBN 1-55105-154-0

   1. Harries, Joyce, 1928– 2. Alberta—Biography. I. Title.
FC3675.1.H37A3 2000   971.23'03'092   C00-910824-6
F1078.25.H37A3 2000

Editorial Director: Nancy Foulds
Project Editor: Lee Craig
Production Manager: Jody Reekie
Book design, layout & production: Heather Markham
Cover Design: Robert Weidemann
Illustrations: Shelley Wales
Cover Photograph: Joyce Harries at 25, modelling photo
Separations & Film: Elite Lithographers Co.
All photographs are from the Harries' family collection and are used with the permission of Joyce Harries, except for the photo on p. 90 by Tamara Eder.

We acknowledge the financial support of the Government of Canada through the Book Publishing Industry Development Program (BPIDP) for our publishing activities.

COMMITTED TO THE DEVELOPMENT OF CULTURE AND THE ARTS

PC: P6

dedication

For my children, Bruce, Jody, Lori, Jeffrey and Daniel,
all my grandchildren and especially remembering
Hu, Tommy and my parents.

acknowledgements

I wish to thank the following people, for their
encouragement and prodding: Edna Alford,
Jack Bilsland, Di Brandt, Lee Craig, Mary Dawe,
Caterina Edwards, Paul Fox, Nancy Foulds, Mel Hurtig,
Margaret Macpherson, Heather Markham, Susan Mayse,
Eunice Scarfe, Judy Schultz, Shirley Serviss,
my children and my friends.
I'd also like to thank Shelley Wales, for her sensitive
drawings, the Alberta Foundation for the Arts, for making
me feel my work is worthwhile,
and Grant and Shane Kennedy, of Lone Pine Publishing,
for taking a chance.

Joyce with her mother Ethel Farrell, 1932

contents

Girdles and Other Harnesses   9
I Have Known (memoir)
photo from modelling days,
circa 1952

I've Decided How I Want My   12
105th Birthday Celebrated if
Cost is No Object (essay)

Then and Now (memoir)   13
photo of Bruce Farrell,
circa 1920s

Tattoo Words (poem)   17

Tea Leaves (memoir)   18

Old Enough to Know (fiction)   21

Apricots (food essay   26
with recipes)

Stampede Cattle Station   33
(memoir)
photo of the Harries family,
around 1971
photo of the Harries family
on horseback
photo of Hu Harries in a
cutting horse contest

The Kidnapping Kid   45
(memoir)

All Gingered Up   46
(food essay with recipes)

October Contentment (poem)   48

Romance at Windsor (memoir)   50
photo of Hu Harries at
Windsor Castle

Nighttime (memoir)   54
formal family photo
photo of Hu and Joyce Harries
with Pierre Elliott Trudeau

Coming Home (essay)   62

Two Seen as One (poem)   65

Her Kitchen Was Her Studio   66
(memoir)
photo of Harries children

The Bluebottle Fly (memoir)   83

Fishing (essay)   85

An Audrey Story (fiction)   86

How to Move A Widow   91
(memoir)
photo of Joyce's family home

Message From My Muse (poem)   99

contents

Tommy (memoir)   101

So Much for Cyrano   102
(fiction)

The First Time (memoir)   105
photo of Joyce in 1945

A Lemon Lover Remembers   106
(food essay with recipes)

Evening in Paris (memoir)   111

Composition for Keith   113
(poem)

Magazine Tracking (essay)   114

It All Worked Out for   116
the Best (memoir)
engagement photos of Hu and Joyce

Dollhouse (memoir)   118

My Mother Told Me   120
(memoir)

The Cuckoo Clock at   121
Aunt Maud's

What Mothers Don't Know   122
(memoir)

The Wedding (fiction)   124

Grandmother Spends   132
Part of the Day at the Lake
(memoir)

I Don't Much Like (essay)   134

Shepherd's Pie (memoir)   137
photo of Hu Harries

Some Days (memoir)   146

Stroll of Poets at the   148
Upper Crust Cafe (poem)

Footprints on the Wall   150
(memoir)

The Cherries Are Ripe   153
(food essay with recipes)

Water (poem)   155

The Ten Dollar Bet (fiction)   156

Where Are You? (poem)   159

Mother (memoir)   160
photo of Joyce's mother's family

The Year We Had Hens   162
at Hidden Bar Ranch (memoir)

My Father's Father (memoir)   163
*photo of the Farrell family,
early 1900s*

contents

Thin Ice Skaters (fiction)   164

Tweezered Words (poem)   166

Welsh Magic (memoir)   167

Feather Boas (poem)   168

Vineyard Dreams (memoir)   170

Northern Lights (memoir)   172

My First Crush (memoir)   173

The Missing Belt Buckle   174
(memoir)

When I Was Little (memoir)   176

As Though to a Child (poem)   185

The Dinner (fiction)   186

A Farmers' Market (fiction)   188

Fluttering Words (memoir)   193
*photo of Joyce, her mother,
dad and dog*

Four-Leaf Clovers (memoir)   196

I Care (poem)   198

No Rhubarb about Rhubarb   199
(food essay with recipes)

When I Think of It All   203
(poem)

One Thing Leads to Another   204
(food essay with recipes)

Old Skin (poem)   207

Pickers' Cookies and Tea   208
(poem)

Sixty-nine-Year-Old Me   210
Talking to My Body (essay)

Slow on the Uptake (poem)   212

This Year, Next Year,   213
Sometime, Never (essay)

Those of Us Who (essay)   214

My Fabulous Fantasy Meal   216
(essay)

I Mustn't (memoir)   220

The Food Grinder (memoir)   221

A Recovered Widow (poem)   223
*photo of Joyce and Hu,
early 1980s*

girdles

and other harnesses
I have known

In the beginning, I'm told, I wore a "belly band" to keep from rupturing when I cried.

Then, in the winter, when I was a little girl living in a northern city, I wore a waist: a reinforced, sleeveless vest of white cotton that had long elastic garters dangling from it, fore and aft. The garters held up white or beige, ribbed woollen stockings. When I bent over, the back garters stretched to their limit, pulling my stockings up so tight at the top of my legs that my heels rose as though yanked by puppet strings, and the front garters loosened and the stockings' knees bagged like baby elephant skin. The space between the stockings' top and my white cotton panties was covered with long, navy, fleece-lined bloomers, which had a pocket on the front for a hankie. If you laughed too hard ploughing through the snowdrifts on your way home from school and wet your panties, the navy in the bloomers ran, and Monday's wash needed extra bleach.

The next piece of feminine harness I wore was a peach-coloured garter-belt. Now, instead of pressure on the shoulders as suffered with the waist, a garter-belt had to be tight enough not to slide over my hipless body and gouge the skin. It was worn over panties and under long, pink woollies.

My mother wouldn't let me have a girdle, but the Christmas when I was twelve and badly wanted one, an understanding Aunt Floss gave me my first. It was a peach-coloured, soft elastic tube, with short, not long, garters.

Another feminine harness was for a different purpose, although it was also made from elastic and was adjustable and had white clips of a different design. The sanitary napkin belt was in my wardrobe, off and on, for thirty-five years.

The next garment—one of real torture—was a long-legged, strongly elasticized panty-girdle. Short garters inside, halfway up the legs, were turned next to the skin with the rubber buttons facing inward, leaving four round, pink imprints on my thighs' backs and fronts. By wearing these garters, I avoided bumps from showing through my pink ecru, lace-trimmed slip, which I wore under slinky, slithery dresses. Even the side seam lines imprinted my skin from waist to above the knee, like a two-striped zebra. Scar-like, red crescents from the pressure of the uplifted, padded brassiere under my 32-A breasts contributed to the assortment of marks on my body.

Then there were the bustiers—for wearing under strapless gowns. A woman needed a black one and a white one. The bustiers had stays: narrow, hard plastic strips in hidden seams that enabled the garment to stand alone on a table. I let my breath out while I fastened it down the front with hooks and eyes. Crescent wires and discrete crescent pads, in the lower bust cups, pushed what little there was to new heights. The rest of my top region was squeezed to such a extent that long, deep breaths were impossible. The bottom of this lace-trimmed contraption met up with the panty-girdle at the waist. Bending back to straighten stocking seams was torture.

Now, when I get out of a shower, what I see is pretty bad, but I console myself in knowing that at least I don't have four button marks on my thighs, stripes down my sides or two crescent welts under my boobs.

The next contraption of horror, if you can believe this, was a pink rubber girdle, a heavier weight than my other girdles and lined like kitchen rubber gloves. It had air holes in a diamond pattern on the front and back, which were supposed to provide air circulation. Often, friends had to help one another roll it off, at the end of a fashion show. You know what rubber gloves are like? It was much worse to wear. Think of trying to slink or walk jauntily down a ramp with a smile on your face, while wearing a push-up, padded bra, a rubber, sweat-inducing girdle, uncomfortable nylons and high-heel shoes usually half a size too small. This demonstration came after we'd been subjected to a too-hot hair dryer with metal curlers, which either curled or straightened but could scorch, especially behind our ears, even though the ears were protected with squares of toilet-paper tissue on two hot clips. And then there were the false eyelashes, whose glue often made our eyes water.

However, one day in the mid-fifties, our modelling club brought in an Italian model from New York, to give us the latest tips on runway modelling and photo shoots. She introduced us to panty-hose, Sears Clingalong, and we were freed. We felt as though we were skinny-dipping. We stopped wearing girdles and stockings, wired bras and false eyelashes. We spread the word.

It must have been the same as when flappers bobbed their hair, took off their corsets, and wore short skirts.

Ahh…comfort. Finally. □

If love is blind, why is lingerie so popular?

—Anon.

I've Decided How I Want My 105th Birthday Celebrated If Cost Is No Object

I want to wear a pale pink Fortuny dress, which may be obtained, I think, at the Metropolitan Museum in New York. If that proves impossible, a pale pink silk dress with a matching cashmere cardigan will do. I'll be so tiny by then, any small size will fit.

I want as many of my descendants as possible there, all of whom, I hope, will be on speaking terms with one another.

I want to hold a very young baby—a blood relative—and nuzzle its neck.

I want three silver buckets of full-blown fragrant roses: one bucket filled with pink roses, one with white and one with yellow.

I want the following in good-looking containers, not jam jars: a tiny bunch of forget-me-nots, some sweet peas, three branches of oncidium orchids and three branches of white, double lilacs.

I want one basket of newly mown hay to smell, one basket of dried leaves to smell, a bowl of freshly dug earth to feel and a lump of fresh bread dough to knead.

I want someone playing the piano softly but loud enough that I can hear George Gershwin, Cole Porter, Duke Ellington and Franz Schubert's piano sonata in B-Flat Major.

I'd also like to hear "Stardust," "Away in a Manger," "Oh Canada" and "Four Strong Winds"—this last song because Ian Tyson sang it at my husband Hu's funeral.

Before dinner I want one very small glass of single malt Scotch with water and no ice. Next, I'd have two tablespoons of Beluga caviar with half a glass of the best champagne. Then I'd have one cup of very strong, hot chicken broth with cold, chopped green onions in it and enough salt, along with one-quarter slice of homemade herb bread with real butter (if such a thing still exists). Finally, I'd like a warm baked-custard that's neither overcooked nor watery, with fresh ripe apricots poached in sugar, water and vanilla bean, served with a double thimbleful of Château d'Yquem—unless British Columbia produces something close by the year 2033, which I would prefer, out of loyalty to the Canadian wine industry.

I don't want a birthday cake, but I want everyone to drink a toast to me and all my relatives and friends, alive and dead, with Krug Grande Cuvée champagne.

If all of this celebrating kills me, please bury my ashes with my first son Tommy and my husband Hu, except for one teaspoon of me that I would like dropped in a good second-hand bookstore. □

then
and now

Photo: My dad, Bruce Farrell

When I was four years old I did not think of danger or consequences. Now I have a hard time not thinking about them.

One hot summer day when I was four, I took my friends, three-year-old Daurel and five-year-old Audrey, to visit my daddy at work. We travelled from across the street from the University of Alberta hospital, east through Garneau, down the then-gravelled Walterdale Hill and over the Fifth Street Bridge. (On the bridge when Audrey and my dog Peter Pug were looking down at the sluggish North Saskatchewan River, Audrey stated reassuringly that she could swim if she fell through the railings.) Then the four of us went up McDougall Hill and across Jasper Avenue to the McLeod Building. We must have been terribly hot and tired by this time, because the total distance was at least two and a half miles.

I took them to the ninth floor on the elevator operated by my friend, black and gold uniformed Mike, who sat on a stool all day, greeted most people by name, opened and closed the black metal accordion doors, and pulled on the heavy brass lever, which stopped the lift at the designated floor.

I could barely open the Farrell Agencies' heavy office door, so we all pushed.

"Where's your mummy, dear?" daddy asked, when I and my little troupe sauntered into his inner sanctum.

"At home, I guess."

I remember him reaching quickly across piles of pink and white insurance papers, for the tall, black phone with its dangling headpiece, his finger fast dialling round and round—33613—our home number. All the while he stared at me with glittering blue eyes and a stern face: "You'd think she could keep track of one four-year-old" and "I'd better get you all right home, she's probably out looking for you. *Whatever* possessed you to come all the way here on your own?"

It was so long ago I don't remember what happened next, except that not unexpectedly our mothers were out child-searching. As so often is the case, children do move quickly and disappear easily when they get even the smallest of headstarts.

Pound for pound, episode for episode, I have not been as adventurous as I was then until lately, when I began exploring what's in my memory. □

The greatest mistake in life is to be continually fearing you will make one

—Elbert Hubbard (1886–1915).

TATTOO WORDS

Angry words do not fade.

They are tattoos

red, blue

permanent.

Hidden but not forgotten.

tea *leaves*

I didn't know what would happen. Of course, no one can see into the future, though my Aunt Floss always claimed she could when she read the tea leaves in the special cup of tea she served me when I was visiting.

I had to drain the liquid so when she turned the cup upside down and rotated it three times while I made a wish, there wasn't a lot of lapsang souchong left floating in the saucer; it was supposed to remain on the cup's bottom and sides. I really didn't like the smoky taste of my aunt's tea—much preferring my nanny's plain black tea—but it was worth drinking to see Aunt Floss's face get dreamy-like. Her glasses would slide down her nose, and she spoke in a trance-like whisper when she told my fortune.

Anyway, as I recall it these sixty years later, she would look seriously at the tea leaves and she always saw a bluebird. She would tell me that I was going to travel and that I liked to dance and that I liked green gherkin pickles, which was no great news, and that I was going to have a happy life, so I guess maybe she could see into the future. But she never said anything about starting to be a writer when I was sixty-seven, and she didn't give me any advice so that I might have started writing sooner. If she could see into the future, she might have suggested I read great books instead of the ordinary stuff like *Anne of Green Gables*, the Elsie Dinsmore series and *The Girl of the Limberlost*.

She would have been surprised, I think, if she could see me now at my computer, thrusting to the back of my head for memories of her: her Bible by her bed; knitting and pattern books beside her chair next to the radio; seed and rose catalogues on the window shelf next to the rocking chair in her pale green kitchen; her square-fingered hands cutting glazed cherries for her light Christmas cakes; and her quilt-covered dining-room table, where her brothers' and sisters' families would gather for non-alcoholic poker sessions, with overflowing ashtrays, smoky air and pennies, nickels and dimes in the winner's pots. She would sit in a creaking wicker chair on her south-facing, glassed-in front porch in Garneau, reading the fat, maroon *Reader's Digest* condensed books that she gave me to zip through when I was older.

Now I'm addicted to books and words. I've joined a book club where we "do" the Great Books' series and every other week read essays from them or old and current bestsellers.

Sometimes I think I'll go back to these books. I will take out the bright pink slivers of "post-its," which mark the pages where I like a word, a phrase or an idea. They will be my tea leaves, to be twirled three times each day, after my second cup of morning coffee. I shall will them to tell me hints of stories and of the future. They will twig my thoughts to travel in my own Walter Mitty way, and who knows what will appear on my pages?

And if Aunt Floss is looking down, she'll say, "I always said you were going to travel and be happy." □

Old Enough to Know

I'm glad I'm old enough to know because now I can understand. If I'd learned of this interesting situation when I was sixteen, I might have jumped off the High Level Bridge. I was pretty self-centred in those days—at home, cranky, with a dying mother, although I really didn't think she would die. My father also tried to deny what he must have known was the near inevitable: that his wife would die before reaching her forty-third birthday.

I heard the story at the funeral of my mother's best friend, Natasha MacDonald. My brother and I called her Aunt Tash, even if she wasn't our real aunt, and we called her husband, who died ten years ago, Uncle Billy. Aunt Tash had a fast and fatal heart attack, the kind that usually happens to hard-driving men past their mid-life crises, not to a healthy eighty-five-year-old woman who had just hit her second hole-in-one on the back nine.

I can't believe it's been forty-five years since Mother died, at forty-two, when I was sixteen. I'm now sixty-one. So much has happened—Mother died, then Father, then Uncle Billy and last year, my brother Jack. However, Aunt Tash just kept on going.

When I was young, Aunt Tash and Uncle Billy lived across our back alley, and Aunt Tash was in our kitchen, it seemed, almost as much as our mother was. When mother was in the last stages of her illness, it was Aunt Tash who was in charge, not my father. Uncle Billy often hovered on the back porch with his oversized blue coffee mug, which had its own hook on the wall next to our stove. He didn't go to work at 8:15 and return at 5:45 like my banker father did. Billy was a writer, and he worked in a converted garage that was attached to his and Tash's house. Uncle Billy was the one who always chuckled hardest at whatever my mother said. He made kites for us with greased brown paper and took us up to the hill behind the university, where we weren't allowed to go by ourselves until we were judged "old and responsible enough" by both my parents. I can't imagine what they feared, except that the trail to the hill cut through the university farm, and maybe they worried a scholarly bull would take a run at us. They rarely provided reasons for their edicts, just "No, you can't."

When I was married the first time, Aunt Edna, Mother's older sister, who played the role of "next-best-thing-to-mother-of-the-bride," told me that I had the same kind of energy my mother had been famous for. She said, "That mother of yours didn't sleep when she was a baby, and when she was a teenager she could slide out our bedroom window and sneak in before the rooster crowed and still look better than the rest of us girls put together. Butter wouldn't melt in her mouth at the breakfast table, where she'd yawn and stretch, toss that kinky black hair of hers and say what a wonderful sleep she'd had and tell us some complicated dream about a cornfield and a green truck with Rudy Vallee singing 'Your Time is My Time' and the 'Whiffenpoof Song,' until Dad would tell her to keep quiet and just eat. She was a *corker* she was."

That was my mother when she was young in the small town of Poplar Meadows.

I knew what she was like when my brother and I were growing up. She was fun and loved word jokes. Puns peppered her sentences, and we would roar with laughter when she would ask us, "Have you ever seen a horse fly? or a ski jump?

or a mouse trap? or a vegetable stand?" and "How do you make an elephant stew?…Keep it waiting for two hours." She saw the funny side of things, which my father didn't. All in all, he wasn't a very demonstrative man, at least with his family. He hated dogs and loved cats. He would lift one of our noisy Siamese, and with a loud smacking kiss say, "How are we today, my beauty?" I don't ever remember him being that loving in public with my mother. He seemed to like solitary pursuits, like stamp collecting, which I hated because you had to sit still and not bump the table.

My mother tried to teach Jack and me to dance, to jitter-bug, when we needed to know. *She* knew, she said, from watching the movies. If she was required to partner Fred Astaire, she claimed, she probably could do that, too. I always hoped to inherit her self-confidence. She had a great sense of rhythm and would flash around the dining-room floor with "Take the A Train" blaring from the record player in the living room. Jack couldn't catch on. She said he had two left feet like his father, though he was so handsome he would appeal to girls just by batting his gorgeous, thick eyelashes and grinning at them. She said I was a natural dancer, and that any good dancer would be thrilled to hold me in his arms, to spin and twirl me. She was right. Somehow I always managed to have a wonderful time on the dance floor, whether the poor boobs were good dancers or not—they all thought they were when they danced with me. I owe something else to her, as well. She said, "Just kid them along," and I knew she meant, "Just enjoy them all, whatever their strengths and weaknesses." And so I did. Maybe that's why I've been married four times, always happily. But we won't talk about all the times I *didn't* marry.

My mother was known for her fine hand-rolled hems, embroidered table runners, bridge cloths and antimacassars.

Although she knew all sorts of fancy stitches, she wasn't good at basic mending, such as splitting worn-out sheets down the middle and sewing the side seams together. Mother was also a cushion fanatic, the more fantastic the better: we had cushions to prop behind us on couches, porch swings, rocking chairs, beds and floor corners, as well as cushion seats on dining-room chairs, hearths, car seats, piano stools, treehouse benches and bicycle seats. In the creation of these cushion wonders, she used silk threads, fine and thick wools, linen threads, ribbons, shells and bugle and seed and coral beads. I could never describe her colour combinations, though they reminded me of silk sunsets, billowing Northern Lights and Las Vegas pyrotechnics.

Mother called Aunt Tash her "little cushion-Russian," because it was she who would take yet another finished, stitched cushion canvas to cover a feather-filled, blue-striped ticking cushion. I remember her oohing and awing, "For sure, Liz, this is my all-time favourite, for sure."

Mother would beam and ask her, "Do you want it Tashy?"

"No, darling. Only for my birthday, remember?"

Some days later, Uncle Billy would deliver another fat cushion to join the piles already on every surface possible, and Mother would give him a hug and a kiss, as though he had done the finishing touches himself. I thought she overdid it sometimes.

I still have a collection of her cushions as well as a Christmas tree skirt, my Christmas stocking and one very tea-stained tea-cozy. They should properly be in a museum, but I use them, just as she did. I've often wished I had one of the good-luck bride's garters she sometimes made, though perhaps I formed my own good luck just thinking about my mother on each wedding day.

So you can imagine my feelings, when, in a rather dusty corner of the church hall, after Aunt Tash's funeral, my Aunt Edna let slip, I now think intentionally, what I had never even suspected all those years ago. She said, "That Tash was a saint, an utter saint. Maybe a foolish one. Who but she would share her husband with her best friend just because the friend's husband couldn't stand his wife's suddenly flat, scarred chest? There must have been something going on before your mother's illness."

My tea cup rattled in its saucer. "Aunt Edna, I don't believe this."

"It's true. Remember that October when your mother was on her last downward slide and I came to help? Your mother told me. She did. Truly. I felt sorry for your father; he was always such a stick, could never keep up with her, but of course that must have been what he found attractive about her."

And she took a large bite out of an egg-salad sandwich on white.

Then I remembered when Mother started making the same two cushions over and over, with only slight variations. The same colours, though different shades, and different sizes. One cushion always had a border of tiny, bright blue cubes, a background of a smiling sun, or sometimes it looked like sunflowers, and golden bugle-beads radiating like fireworks over all. The other cushion always had a black border, floating, green, oblong shapes and crystal beads that rained downwards. Maybe the sunny blue and sparkling gold one was for Uncle Billy and the other for my banker father, with its border in black and its greenbacks and tears. □

Apricots

I can't believe fruit can be so bright—like techni-coloured raspberries in the back lane, only on trees in our orchard—higher, bigger, brighter. Usually, the brighter the color is, the sweeter the fruit.

I take a hammer and go out back on the cement side-walk to bang the apricot pits, extracting the fat baby-almond so safely hidden inside its super-tough shell. Meanwhile, the fruit, sugar and lemon juice are cooking on the stove as part of my preparations to make jam. Some of the pits are in frag-ments, and some are whole. I rush the fragments back to the spitting jam pot and put a whole kernel in each jar. I taste and test the thick nectar and finally pour it into the jars and seal with hot caps and rings. I line the jars up along the window sill overlooking the bay. A hummingbird is interested, and a cone falls from the ponderosa pine, and I say, "Amen." I write and date the labels, stick them on the shiny jars, and think, *I wonder whose breakfast toast this will slather?*

At friends John and Miriam's in Paris, Hu and I had an old-fashioned, grainy apricot tart that was superb, but the much simpler and healthier apricot clafouti is what I choose to make (see recipe, p. 28). It's faster and has a similar taste,

Old age is a lot of crossed off names in an address book

—Anon.

though a different texture. Just put the easily pitted and sugared apricots, with almonds, into a greased dish, whisk the other ingredients, and pour over. Bake and then grill briefly with added brown sugar. Mmm, it smells wonderful! Serve it warm with fresh mint on the side. You can guild the lily if you sprinkle it lightly with either kirsch or Cointreau.

Dressings containing dried apricots have a real affinity for lamb, duck or chicken. Chewing lovely, leathery apricots on the job is allowed if you're the cook. Just don't eat handfuls and then drink five cups of tea, or you'll have one big stomachache like one of my sons did when he was very young.

The chutney (p. 31) is a sweet-and-sour treat, for serving with crackers, cheese or meat. Because fresh salsa, with its hot-hot component, has become trendy, now beating sales of ketchup, poor old apricot chutney must wait its turn to come back as an old-fashioned favourite. It will, and I will still be there making it, if only so I can stand in my bathing suit, covered with an apricot-stained apron, bare feet sticking to the sugary floor, stirring with my long-handled wooden spoon and inhaling the pungent perfume of sun-soaked apricots, onions, brown sugar, vinegar, garlic, raisins, walnuts, fresh ginger and spices.

The Recipes

Apricot Clafouti (6 servings)

4 1/2 c. pitted, halved, ripe apricots
1/3 c. sugar
1/4 c. flaked almonds
3 eggs
1 c. milk
1/2 c. all-purpose flour
2 tsp. pure vanilla
1/4 tsp. salt
2 tbsp. packed brown sugar

In a bowl, toss apricots with almonds and half the sugar. Place in concentric circles on a greased 10" fluted porcelain tart dish or glass pie plate.

In a separate bowl, whisk together the remaining white sugar with milk, flour, vanilla and salt until smooth. Pour over fruit.

Bake in 350° F oven until puffed and set (about 40–50 minutes).

Sprinkle with brown sugar. Broil about 3 minutes or until dark. Serve warm if possible.

Apricot Bulgar Stuffing

(for lamb, duck or chicken)

1 med. onion, chopped
1/4 c. butter
1 3/4 c. bulgar (cracked wheat)
1 1/4 c. stock (lamb, duck or chicken)
1 tbsp. pine nuts or blanched almonds
8 whole dried apricots, cut into strips
1/8 c. butter* (may leave out)

Soften onion in butter. Stir in bulgar, and keep stirring over low heat for about 10 minutes. Add stock, nuts and apricots.

Cover and simmer until the liquid is absorbed (about 10 minutes).

* Stir in extra butter and, with a tea towel over the pan's top, put on the lid and cook very low for up to 20 minutes.

Duck, lamb or chicken can be stuffed with some of this stuffing. The rest should be reheated and served on the meat platter.

Apricot Jam

2 lbs whole apricots (firm but ripe)
1 c. water
juice of 1 lemon
4 c. sugar

Cut the apricots in half and remove the pits. Crack half the stones and remove the kernels. Set aside.

Put apricots in jam kettle with water and lemon juice. Bring to boil and simmer until the fruit is soft. Stir in sugar until dissolved. Boil rapidly.

Add kernels when close to jam-setting stage.

Skim and pour into jars. Seal, following manufacturer's directions for jam making.

Apricot Chutney

1/2 c. chopped onion
1 1/3 c. raisins
3 cloves garlic, chopped
8 c. pitted apricots, sliced in eighths
2/3 c. shredded fresh ginger
1 c. broken walnuts
2 tbsp. chili powder
2 tbsp. mustard seeds
1 tbsp. salt
4 c. cider or white vinegar
3 1/3 c. brown sugar

Mix all of the ingredients together and bring to a boil.

Turn down heat and simmer 1 hour or longer, until mixture thickens and turns a rich brown color. Stir frequently to prevent scorching.

Pour into sterilized jars and process according to manufacturer's directions for jam making. □

stampede

cattle station

I would hear him say, "I need to own land." At that time in my life, during the early 1950s, I don't think I realized what this need would result in. He didn't mean the lot under our city house—he meant *real* land. Surely, it was a bred-in-the-bone need, born of a Welsh immigrant father's need to do the same. And so, setting off a chain of events I could not have foreseen, my husband Hu bought what we could barely afford: 100 acres of "gumbo" and "grey-wooded" land, east of Edmonton.

Then we bought a pony and more land, including a settler's cabin, a tractor, a post pounder, posts, barbed wire coils, a well driller's time and a few head of cattle. Hu's veterinarian father had loved black Aberdeen Angus cattle, so we had to have some of those, too.

Next came the commercial Herefords—those splashy brown and white cattle we branded with Hu's father's long unused brand—H, attached B and a bar underneath. From this design, we "cleverly" named our property the Hidden Bar Ranch, even though the bar underneath wasn't hidden. (Hell's Bells was the only other name we could come up with.) Then we needed corrals, a weigh-scale, a neck squeeze, a grain crusher and a building to house it, a barn, the well driller again and a veterinarian's phone number. I was learning, as was our banker.

Watching my first branding, and listening to the men's quiet cursing, including Hu's, at the branding chute, I thought, *Ooh, that smell—it's not just smoke, whoo—the sizzle—no wonder the steer's bawling.* (By then I'd learned the difference between heifers, steers, heifer calves, bull calves, cows and bulls.) *C'mon now, you have to get used to it and so will the children*, I'd think. And another HB bar would be imprinted on a huffing critter's left rump. Then it would be released from the neck squeeze and scramble to join its unhappy companions.

I knew Hu liked the look of the Angus—the black "blockiness" of them, strung out against a summer sky. He also liked that their cows were good mothers and that their meat was well-marbled. Because they were purebreds, the Angus weren't branded. Instead, they had ear tattoos made when their ears were scrunched with a contraption that had rotating number dials. The ears were also quickly pierced with green, white-numbered tags for fast identification. Each animal had "papers" that had to be applied for from either the Canadian or American registries.

Meanwhile, I would be exploring the nearby woods, three minutes from the cabin. In spring, I would plunder and rationalize, *There are tons of these Saskatoon blossoms, and I'll just take enough for the weekend.* Their stiff branches would sit in a quart sealer, baby leaves the color of limes, May-fragrant petals dropping on the table.

Later, I would crawl behind the cabin, seeking two-inch stocks of pink wintergreen. I took only a few to put in white egg cups, along with short-stemmed wood violets. Other egg cups held flowers picked by the children—dandelions with bent stems and the odd bluebell with spit bugs dangling.

I may just give them Kraft Dinner with ketchup, canned peaches and bought cookies for dessert, but at least we have table flowers.

From left to right: Joyce, Jeff, Lori, Bruce, with Danny, Jody, Hu

One spring Hu went to a dispersal sale and hooked up with Dave, a smooth talker from Virginia. I didn't meet Dave until after the handshake deal. Together they had bought two cattle-liners of pure-bred black Angus and the first of five farmsteads: 14,000 acres of southern Alberta prairie grass and huge sky that we would call the Stampede Cattle Station. We would have bigger bank loans than we'd ever dreamed would be possible.

If you take the old Macleod Trail out of Calgary and go south to Nanton, you're getting close. The Rockies are on the right, but at the dusty orange grain elevators at Stavely, turn left on a narrow road, and go past shallow, white alkaline lakes, black cattle and miles of barbed wire fence. At the green and white sign—"The Stampede Cattle Station"—you're there.

Sporadically, we would travel the five hours to Stampede, and I would get out of the car at our faded green trailer and think, as I turned around in a full circle, looking up and out, *So quiet. So huge. This sky is surely higher, wider, bluer and more perfect than any sky anywhere else in the world.*

The blowing tumbleweed and grasses were all that moved, save for a few birds and the black cattle in distant pastures. There were no trees, except for a handsome windbreak planted by a pioneer long ago. Water diviners had to be magicians to find water in this land.

With Dave as partner, we then brought in Bob, who had western Canadian roots and was the president of an international investment group. Bob was interested in going to the cattle shows in Toronto, Denver and Louisville and perhaps getting his photo taken in the winner's circle.

I used to shake my head in wonderment, thinking, *The amount of money that flows in is amazing but more surprising is what flows out and I probably don't know the half of it.*

We had horses and tack enough for a dozen cowboys and a show team of five people housed in Washington, Indiana. Jim and his crew were University of Pennsylvania grads—hardworking, dedicated young men who transported and looked after the show string and helped give us an important name in the world of black Aberdeen Angus cattle.

One year we had the Grand Champion female at the Toronto Royal and the Reserve Champion at the Denver show. I was in Denver that year with Hu. I remember going with Herman Purdy, professor emeritus, from the University of Pennsylvania, to a restaurant with a pile of shrimp in the middle of the table, and he had to show me how to peel them the right way. Today, I wouldn't be embarrassed, but I was then.

I didn't know yet that our lives would pour and dribble into many other venues, and that the cattle that were in four places—the show string in Indiana, the unit at the newly

36

acquired Paradise Ranch in B.C., a few hundred at Hidden Bar Ranch and the bulk here at Stampede—would be lost.

Hu's quest to have a ten-horse hitch to take to cattle shows would also prove to be a financial drain. We eventually ended up with an eight-horse hitch of palomino-coloured Belgian horses, a shiny red show wagon emblazoned in gold printing with our Stampede logo, a full-time driver and a truck and a trailer to haul the whole thing to parades and contests.

I thought, *There appears to be a pattern here, but Hu's so enthusiastic, he's like a kid—he must know what he's doing. I love him. So how can I have doubts?* However, I still felt the publicity value of this circus was hardly worth the trouble and expense—but I felt like a kill-joy whenever I said anything to my husband.

I didn't want to think about a few years earlier: rodeos twice-produced in Toronto at the Maple Leaf Gardens and once at the Maple Leaf ballpark had been exciting but financially catastrophic. For the first performance, people stayed away in droves—they were glued to their T.V.s, because John F. Kennedy had just been assassinated. The next two tries, while better, were also money guzzlers.

In many ways, I looked forward to our yearly production sales, always held during the week of the Calgary Stampede. I can recall one time so clearly—I don't know which sale day it would have been, but I was lying in the green trailer with my eyes open. Early morning sun streamed through the high window, making a light warm stripe filled with dust particles across the bed and the grey linoleum floor. The rumpled green quilt had been pushed to the bottom of the bed. Hu had got up a while ago, and a formerly sweat-soaked sheet, though now dry, was pulled up to my chin to keep a bit of warmth in my bones. The early morning trailer still retained the night's coolness.

Hu had gone to meet Hans, our ranch foreman, but first he kissed me good-bye.

"Sleep longer, darling. We won't be in for breakfast for more than an hour at least."

I had smiled and turned over, waiting for his heavy footsteps to disappear and the swaying of the trailer to stop, but only temporarily, demonstrating the impermanence of our lives at the Stampede Cattle Station. It was as though Hu had stepped off the edge of the world, and I was alone, with the hum of the fridge motor, a dripping tap and the loud sound of nothing.

Following breakfast in the trailer, Hu would be all smiles, though I recognized that pinched look on his face when he didn't think he was being watched. Then he would be in the yard by the picnic table, where Lloyd, our sales manager, and his partner, Doug, would be pencilling figures on the back of cigarette packages and around the edges and backs of our sale catalogues. They'd be getting pre-sale bids, either on the phone or in person, from prospective bidders. Much laughter, handshaking and toasting would occur after the sale, although everyone was in a hurry to "Wrap it up."

In the trailer, I'd be thinking my instructions to myself: *Sandwiches—hope there's enough ham and Grey Poupon left. Pop more ice. Use the bathroom before the men come back in to use the phone again. Sweep the floor. Don't say much—just listen.*

Unmailed copies of our catalogue, which Lloyd and Doug produced, were in boxes in the sale barn. The glossy pages were filled with our cattle's extended bloodlines, show results and other "positive" copy, along with pictures of the cattle taken weeks before by a "cattle photographer," whose helpers brushed, sprayed and entertained the beasts so they would look handsomely alert for the camera. (It all would have been done with the same quick attention that fashion photographers devote to models during runway shoots.)

Lloyd and Doug arranged for extra sale ring callers, as well as helpers in the back pens and trucking and border-crossing arrangements for buyers after the sale.

Well over 100 people, including a small busload of Hutterite neighbours, there for the food and entertainment value only, would sit on bleachers in the big barn. A silver-tongued "colonel" from Virginia would, with a partner, admonish the buyers: "Don't make me cry, my good folks, this little lady is from Blackbird Dolly by Byergoes Black Revolution. Her full sister was top female at the Toronto Royal, and you're offering me—What did you say in the back row?"

Then that low-pitched spiel of the cattle auctioneer would continue. Finally, with a crash of the gavel and a "Sold, to Gore Farms, of Tennessee," the next animal would be guided into the sale ring as the one just sold would be guided out.

Hu would be pacing to one side, with our boys helping in the pens and our girls helping in the office area. I'd be either pacing (knowing well what was at stake) or—if our neighbours the Ohlers didn't barbecue roasts for us—ready-ing the food for the onslaught after the sale. Remember, these were the days of great meat consumption, when barbecued steaks, roasts and hamburgers were eaten in great quantities by one and all, and only hippies were vegetarians.

It was easy for me to tell if things were going well or not by looking at Hu. Watching Dave was another matter. His face would shine as though this sale was a Sotheby's sale and we had sold a Van Gogh to a buyer from Japan. Originally from Montana, Dave worked as a cattle and horse buyer, and at the time we met he owned and lived at the historic Sugarloaf Farm in Virginia. He was a big man—in stature, voice, laughter and vision. He wore cowboy boots, which made him about six foot eight, and he had to take off his cowboy hat when he entered the trailer at the ranch. He smoked Lucky Strikes and drank either beer or Scotch, because we couldn't get Bourbon easily in those days.

Some years before we met, Dave was on cattle-buying rounds in Saskatchewan, where he discovered and bought a young bull that he prophetically named Colossal. This bull changed the Angus breed in North America: to tall and rangy from the squat critters that even the Queen Mother bred. In the seventeen years Dave was our partner, he had his ups and

downs, just as we did. He lost Sugarloaf. His wife divorced him. He had a heart attack, married his nurse and moved to New Zealand. He won the biggest race in New Zealand with a horse he had raised, lost all that and came back to North America, seeking another "find" in the cattle world—another Colossal. Dave was just one of those guys who never quit. No wonder he and Hu liked each other so much.

One time he arrived at the ranch in the battered car we kept at the Calgary Airport just for his occasional visits and said, "Let's go to Claresholm to the 'Flying N' for dinner." After the meal, when it came time to pay, he drawled, "I'll catch it next time—I've only got New Zealand currency." Days later, on his way to one hot deal or another, he'd still have that New Zealand money in his wallet.

I remember the sale of '74, and the thunderstorm that occurred late in the day. Gyp, Hans' dog, whined and crawled on his belly under a wagon. Long, yellow riding slickers were pulled over bright cowboy shirts by everyone, and plastic covers were snapped over expensive straw Stetson hats. Black buckled rubber boots were put on over cowboy boots and not an umbrella was in sight.

After loading the cattle liners and finishing some paper-work in the barn, the men dripped into the trailer. The coffee pot's burbled steam coated the small windows, wilted tiger lilies in a dill pickle jar and kinked my hair. I couldn't help thinking, *I'm as black-furious as that sky out there! Whoo, when the bank hears the sale didn't go like we were so sure it would...We were supposed to have settled our last operating loan and then some.*

And still Hu smiled, but I knew the anxiety behind his eyes. *He's wonderful...how can he, almost year after year...?*

Bruce, Jody, Lori, Jeff and Danny all took their turns working summers at Stampede. The girls riding herd, det-ecting for cows ready for artificial insemination and helping Jeff, when he was one of the technicians. Danny drove equip-ment. Bruce drove the cattle liner and, when younger, worked at Hidden Bar in the summers. We thought these times would add to their "life-experience banks."

It was hard for Hu and Dave, being absentee owners, but we did have people to run the ranch for us.

Slow-talking, tough Tim, who'd worked for Dr. Armand Hammer in Montana, was our first manager at Stampede. Then we hired George, our bank manager in Stavely, as our full-time manager. He and his wife Marnie were great and worked so hard, but it was not the life for them and they moved on. Then we got E.P. Taylor's head cattle man—Jim

42

and his wife, Willa, were from a very small unit at Windfields in Ontario. In the end, we would only have old Hans, with the strength of a bull, and a couple of half-competent helpers, meaning Hu had to journey down to the ranch more often to keep tabs on the welfare of the cattle.

By this time we had bought out Bob and Dave, although we could ill-afford it. Hu's economic consulting practice was acting like a young cash cow for the ranches and more lately, for the coast-to-coast horse vanning company we'd become entangled in. We even manufactured our own semi-trailers in a shop out at Hidden Bar Ranch, until a fire destroyed it, along with our machine shop.

I often wondered, *What would we be doing if Hu hadn't travelled some of the roads he did? The ranches, the trucking company, the turned-down pipeline application, the chemical company, the trailer factory, the charcoal plant, the pipemill company, the Faculty of Commerce, the law school, the Liberal Party and a four-year stint in Ottawa under Prime Minister Trudeau and starting a new western political party called "The National," the party preceding Mel Hurtig's party of the same name.* And we were still converting the ranch in B.C. to more vineyards when he died.

At least he didn't talk me into selling French-fried bananas on the summer fair circuit—a momentary idea in our first year of married life, which we dropped.

Ideas spouted from Hu like bubbles in a boiling corn pot. He was never more alive than when he was pacing around the kitchen telling me what could be next. I've heard it said, "A man has to do what a man has to do," and I was not a stick-handling kind of wife, just one who cheered or cried inwardly from the bleachers.

Nor did I plan on ageing alone. I was to have floated through this time of life, still a cherished woman, made to feel

Hu near the end of a three-minute ride in a cutting horse contest

youthful by a generous, courtly man. I was to have a lifetime companion. I saw us walking into the sunset, hand-in-hand, disappearing over the curve of the earth, as the lights dimmed. The words "The End" would float across the screen, and the music would reach a crescendo, and that would be that.

But I was not to know, in those July days so long ago, that we would lose the Stampede Cattle Station.

Only memories, trophies, black and white cattle photos and one family photo of a sale remain, to remind us of the twenty or so years when we were only small dots under that huge prairie sky. □

The Kidnapping Kid

It's been a secret for many years, but did you know I kidnapped a baby when I was little? I did, and it was so long ago I don't even remember how my mother and I returned it.

One hot afternoon I was supposed to be playing quietly by myself while my mother napped. I decided to go and visit my Aunt Floss, who lived three blocks from our home. I rang her bell, but she was out, so to return home I cut through her back lane, across the backyard of a house where there was a bunch of piled ladders. Just above the ladders was a window, with a curtain hanging out. I looked in, and there in a little bed a dark-haired baby sat, smiling at me. I remembered hearing my mother say something about how the people in this house had too many children. I had wondered what she had meant by that, but at the moment it seemed to make good sense to me to take this extra one—I had been pleading for a baby brother or sister for as long as I could remember.

When I arrived home with this wet-diapered child, my mother was naturally shocked, especially when I said, "Well, you were napping, and you said they had too many and we need one, so I took it!"

I know she hustled me over to the baby's home, but for the life of me I don't know whether we slid the baby through the window back into its own bed or whether we knocked at the door. Anyway, I remained an only child and had to wait many years to have six babies of my own. □

All Gingered Up

"All gingered up" means to be very provoked, while gingering a dish is likely to just provoke smiles.

The simplicity of a fast stir-fry spiked with shreds of fresh, pale ginger lifts the whole mass from a "blah" healthy to a "zippy" healthy. When the temperature plummets, toss a chunk of ginger in a mug of water, microwave one minute and thirty seconds, add a squeeze of lemon and a squirt of honey, and you'll be warm from your scalp to your toes.

A jar of pickled ginger is a great little condiment to have on hand. Find firm, smooth, unwrinkled roots of ginger in your fresh food section (Oriental markets often have the fastest turnover of ginger so theirs is the best quality). It's so easy to use it in your cooking. Just peel about a half-pound of ginger and slice it into paper-thin pieces. Pour boiling water over it and let it sit for two minutes, then drain. Meanwhile, make the brine with 1 1/2 c. plain Japanese rice wine or grain vinegar, 3 tbsp. apple cider vinegar, 2 tbsp. plain distilled vinegar or raspberry vinegar, 1/3 c. sugar and 1 tbsp. kosher salt. Bring to simmer, stirring until sugar and salt are dissolved. Pour over ginger in a sterile jar and refrigerate when cool. This mixture will keep for ages, with the brine becoming cloudy. If you don't need to ration it, a few slices in cream-cheesed crackers, or a few teaspoons chopped and sprinkled on chicken or fish or in salads, will get your tastebuds standing at gentle attention. The leftover juice is marvellous as the acid in your vinaigrettes.

To save a chunk of ginger from withering, put it in a jar of sherry and keep it in the fridge. Your next stir-fry will have shreds of a darker, more mysterious flavour.

Upscale your crabapple jelly by adding chunks of preserved ginger.

The Recipes

Ginger-Mango Salsa

Mix together:
2 tbsp. chopped green onions
2 tbsp. chopped cilantro
1 tbsp. peeled, chopped fresh ginger
2 tbsp. fresh lime juice and the zest of 2 limes
2 tbsp. brown sugar
2 tbsp. fish sauce
1 tbsp. Chinese chili sauce

Dice 2 small mangoes into small chunks and fold them into the salsa.

This salsa will keep refrigerated for two days and may be served with chicken, steak, brown rice or barbecued tofu.

A Hint for Gingered Brownies

Add some chopped crystallized ginger and orange rind as a replacement for some of the nuts in a brownie recipe. □

Peanut butter is a child's paté
—Anon.

OCTOBER CONTENTMENT

I walk the streets of old Garneau
as I did when a child
though now I am alone
with a Walkman.
The same Indian summer smell
spice in my nose, head and bones
soft, warm brown and lingering.

Grey-haired, hunched old-house owners
rake leaves.
I wait to hear creaking-gate sounds
as they bend
pushing armfuls of chipped leaves
into green garbage bags.

Laughing young students
in rented digs
sit on faded porch steps
beer in hand
watching leaves fluttering before them.

A black blotched cat
sits hunched on red shale
under dusty spruce.
Why isn't he stretched in stripes of sun
filtering through leafless caragana?

Flowerbeds are dug,
clods of black soil
wait cold
white eiderdown covers.

Colors today are gold, rust, maroon and brown.

No blue of delphiniums
only sky
where wobbling rows of ducks
silently fly above me.

No yellow of mums,
only a shiny van
Spice Girls shrieking
through open windows.

No orange of nasturtiums,
only T-shirted children
roller-blading around me.

Husky whispers of skittering leaves
tell me
   jump in a pile
   jump in a pile
       jump in a pile.

Leaf crumbs
in my hair,
down my neck
and in my socks
   scratch memories
   of other Indian summers
       when I was young and oblivious.

romance
at Windsor

The warm May fragrance of lilacs mingled with
diesel fumes. I awoke that first morning in the Castle Hotel
in Windsor to the call of a cuckoo bird. Hu and I laughed
after I said, "How odd to have a cuckoo clock in a bedroom."

It was my first trip to England. Hu had been asked to judge Canadian cutting horse contests at the Royal Windsor Horse Show and other county fairs at the invitation of Prince Phillip. We had arrived late in the day, and Hu had pointed out the castle and told me there was much to see. We were to spend that morning and afternoon alone, after a parting of three weeks. Though it is now thirty-seven years later, I still remember moments of that day as though they happened last week.

I remember many details: the hotel bedroom with the rumpled sheets—in three weeks, we had not forgotten one another's bodies; the window overlooking a back parking lot that was bordered with lilac trees in bloom; and the quiet uncalled-for knock on the door by a sweet-faced young woman who brought us tea in bed and started us drinking tea instead of coffee first thing in the morning.

I don't remember much about Windsor Castle though we took tea in a minuscule "grace and favour" home on the castle grounds. The tea was presided over by a charming elderly couple who had served England in some noble way that enabled them to have a cold, cramped place to live, with the most famous address in the world.

I do recall buying a silver coffee spoon with the castle's emblem on it, as well as one that says "Eton."

Hu judging a cutting horse contest at Windsor Castle

We ambled through Windsor for the remainder of the morning, joining throngs of early tourists. We laughed when we saw the boys from Eton in their striped pants and tight jackets that their wrists stuck out from; they were quickly outgrowing their clothes just as our five boys and girls were at home. Hu told me how much he missed us all when he was away on his frequent trips, but we both agreed that these extravagant times stolen from our children were probably what helped our ongoing romance. We were often teased by relatives who said, "Isn't it about time the honeymoon was over?"

Next we wandered into a wine shop, although in those days we were complete wine novices. We talked to a pickle-faced man who looked down his nose at us but still sold us a bottle of glorious red wine, two wine glasses and a wooden-handled corkscrew that I still have.

We found a bakery and a cheese shop, and laden with wine, glasses, corkscrew, bread, Stilton cheese and cheddar cheese, we left the crowded high street, walking along the side of a narrow river. We sat under a huge, spreading oak tree on the riverbank, where the bright green grass was dappled by light coming through the branches. As we ate and drank, the sharp cheeses disappeared, as did the whole bottle of wine. We broke the remaining bread in pieces and threw them to the white swans who had been sailing past us on the river. Eton boys, their longish hair flowing behind them, called to one another as they bicycled past.

There was something about that afternoon—the privacy, although we weren't completely alone, and how we talked about our family, our future and our love for one another. It was a simple meal but unforgettable. □

*An average person laughs about
15 times a day.*

nighttime

When I was five, I hugged my teddy bear and it hummed "Oh where, oh where has my little dog gone?"

At ten, I read *Anne of Green Gables* by flashlight under my bedcovers.

At fourteen, I found blood on my sheets and knew I had become a woman.

At sixteen, I turned my pillow over to the cool side and fell asleep dreaming of the boy who had kissed me goodnight on the front porch.

At sixteen and three-quarters, I lay in bed too excited to sleep. Today, May the eighth, 1945, World War II had ended. My uncle and cousins would come home. I wondered how the war's end would change my little world.

At nineteen, I slid out of bed and stood in the half dark of the honeymoon suite, looking down at my sleeping husband of nine hours. I knew then, like swans, we were life mates.

At twenty, I woke, dazed in my hospital bed, and heard the words of a woman in white: "Mrs. Harries, you have a beautiful eight-pound four-ounce baby boy."

On my twenty-first birthday, I dragged myself out of bed to the nursery, changed, fed, rocked and kissed our still colicky baby, Tommy.

At twenty-one, living in Ottawa, I got up to check on Tommy, who had a leg caught between old-fashioned crib bars. Leaning over, I pulled him into the middle of his bed and covered him up, while stroking his rumpled curls.

At twenty-two, I dragged myself out of bed to the new nursery back in Edmonton, to change, feed, rock and kiss another colicky baby—Bruce.

At twenty-four, I dragged myself out of bed to the nursery, to change, feed, rock and kiss another colicky baby—Jody. And I covered up and kissed two little boys who were in a deep sleep.

At twenty-five, together with Hu, I built a croup tent for Tommy. Brooms and mops held up soggy sheets over his wheezing head. A dangerous hotplate held a big pot of steaming water. We took turns in the tent with him.

Still twenty-five, I lay sobbing in my crying husband's arms. Our four-and-a-half-year-old Tommy had died from polio.

Still twenty-five, I paced our moonlit living room, holding Jody, who was only one year old. I was crying, "Why, why?"

At twenty-six, I dragged myself to Bruce's room and held a waste basket for him to throw up in.

Still twenty-six, in a Quonset hut in Pammel Court at Iowa State University, I kept soda crackers beside the bed, to settle my morning sickness, which was happening at night.

At twenty-seven, I heard the nurse on duty in maternity say, "I can always tell when it's a first baby. The parents are more excited." And so, late at night, Lori arrived. Another colicky baby to keep me up!

At twenty-nine, I knew it would be expedient to have this next baby sometime between Bruce's kindergarten Hallowe'en party and Hu's trip to Ottawa on the first of November. At the nearby university hospital, while goblins roamed outside, Jeffrey arrived—once more, a colicky baby.

Still twenty-nine, I dragged myself to the girls' room and soothed Jody, who had a nightmare about a big, black dog at the bottom of her bed.

At thirty, I slept fitfully on the grey chesterfield. Propped in a sitting position, I was wracked with coughing spells. Buckley's cough syrup was on the coffee table beside me, and fumes of Vick's Vaporub drifted in the cool living-room air. My family, asleep upstairs, would not be disturbed.

At thirty-one, at Hidden Bar Ranch—our place east of Edmonton—in the bed of a small, red trailer, I listened to springs creaking as Hu rolled over. I kept listening for sounds outside, to make sure all was well in the back of the station wagon where Bruce, Jody and Lori were sleeping. Little Jeff slept on the couch on the other side of the low-ceilinged kitchenette. Mosquitoes buzzed around my head. It was impossible for me to sleep.

At thirty-two, I gave birth to the last of our planned babies. I guess I was getting tired. Danny, too, was colicky, especially at night.

At thirty-three, with the phone on my side of the bed, I answered the phone calls about snow removal and bad neighbours or the crank calls from drunks—all to do with Hu's part-time job as a city alderman.

At thirty-six, in Windsor, England, I was awakened in the early morning by the first cuckoo bird I had heard that didn't pop out of a clock. I remembered the dream I had just had, where Hu rode right into the "Member's Tent," while I was taking tea with the Queen. He said, "Hop on, your Majesty. I'll take you for a ride on a Western saddle."

At forty, I lay in bed smiling. We'd won the election. Now what?

At forty-two, I woke up at the Chateau Laurier—where Hu would stay when Parliament was in session—because I could hear the burbling hot-water pipes and the political wannabees who were arguing their way down the hall. I looked out the window at the Peace Tower, and I wondered if we were making a mistake in not moving east to Ottawa.

At forty-four, I heard the drawl of our southern neighbours as they opened the hotel room door across from ours. We'd been at a dinner at the Smithsonian, and, frankly, the wine had been poured too often at our table. We left the party after the chicken dancing.

Also at forty-four, my first night home after a cruise found me fatherless. I didn't get to say good-bye.

At forty-five, I lay in bed beside an unhappy man. Prime Minister Pierre Trudeau's Liberals were "wiped out" in the West, and Hu was one casualty—only one four-year term. He'd learned a lot, but, looking back, I wish he'd never done it. I think he paid dearly in too many exhaustion points.

Still forty-five, at Hidden Bar Ranch, I listened to coyotes howling at the moon. The pump around the corner from our bedroom door clicked and hummed. Molly and Willy, our Old English Sheep Dogs, lapped pool water noisily, and the waterbed sloshed as Hu rolled over.

When I was forty-six, Hu and I pulled the mattress off our bed at Paradise Ranch in southern British Columbia. We dragged it to the porch and fell asleep watching August shooting stars, while bats squeaked and swooped over our heads.

At forty-nine, I answered a call from Toronto with the news that our first grandchild, Billy, had arrived. Would I come down in a couple of days? It was hard to go back to sleep. I knew Jody would be a superb mother, if she channelled her over-abundance of energy wisely.

Me, Hu and Pierre Elliott Trudeau during the 1968 election campaign

At fifty, I heard the lapping of the Adriatic in front of the guest house. Fig tree branches scraped across the bedroom windows, and early morning coffee trays were placed loudly onto stone steps.

At fifty-two, my little mother died while I slept. That night was dreamless. I'd said good-bye but wasn't holding her hand at the moment of her death.

At fifty-four, I lay sleepless next to Hu, thinking about Bruce's brush with death after his cancer surgery earlier that week.

At fifty-seven, I woke from a deep sleep, worrying about the financial pressure Hu was under. I didn't realize how severe it was this time, and besides, he had always surmounted all trouble.

On the night of my fifty-eighth birthday, too much Italian food and red wine disturbed my sleep. Everyone, except for Jody and John, who were at a "birthing class," had sung, "Happy Birthday, dear Mom." We had laughed and laughed, me playing the straight man, as is often the case with Bruce and Jeff.

Two weeks and two days later, I lay with my eyes wide open. I was in Vancouver at cousin Bob's. That morning I had seen Hu die from a massive heart attack while riding his horse, Twister. My mind spun senselessly. The dawn came.

At sixty-one, overtired, I woke in the night on a warm fall evening. Touring slowly through each room of my house, I remembered moving into this home we had built thirty-eight years ago. And I remembered. And I remembered. And I remembered. But I had made the right decision. Packed boxes were piled expectantly, like piles of nursery blocks waiting for someone to tumble them. Today, I would be moving to a new home.

Still sixty-one, I listened to the students' laughter that was wafting through the window in my new home. Half-awake, I turned on the bed lamp, pushed my puffy down pillows in a bigger heap, leaned back and re-opened the book I was reading earlier.

At sixty-three, I couldn't get to sleep at all one night. Lori had been diagnosed with multiple sclerosis. When I talked to her, she said, "The good thing is, it's not life-threatening, it just might spoil my quality of life."

At sixty-seven, I lay in bed smiling. My first piece of creative fiction had been published in the *Edmonton Journal*.

When I was still sixty-seven, I lay exhausted in the smallest bedroom in the house at the Paradise Ranch. I was thinking how few hours I had left to re-energize for the next day. I was running six-day retreats for writers and artists. Mary Dawe, a creative writing teacher, inspired her students, and Toni Onley brought his talent, along with his fat Chinese brushes and his stories, to the retreat. He had also brought a young actress friend who had a Patsy Cline show. She belted out "Crazy," and we had clapped like crazy and drank more Okanagan wine.

At sixty-eight, I lay in bed trying to come up with a way to make money. What could I do to replace the artists' and writers' retreats, because the ranch wasn't going to be available? *The few weddings you do, and your creations at craft fairs and farmers' markets don't pay enough bills. What about writing?*

A week before my seventieth birthday, I lay in bed smiling. I couldn't believe my good fortune—I'd been awarded a junior literary grant from the Alberta Foundation for the Arts!

At seventy, I woke at four-thirty in the morning. I wondered how much longer I could remain in this house, and why none of my children were as happy as I believed I had been at their stage of life. I listened to CBC Overseas Deutshevella and the broadcast from Australia. I snapped the radio off, and thought about what I think about in the night. □

Tell the truth.
There's less to remember

—bumper sticker.

coming *home*

It's not like coming home from a trip with Hu, when the children were little—the door bursting open and so much noise! Then I wished I could turn tail no matter how glad I was to see their jumping little bodies.

This time or rather these times, the door is locked and the house dark. I pay the cabby, and he lifts my suitcases onto the porch. Although the house smells musty and dusty, it still smells like home—friendly enough and familiar. With relief, I think of my soft bed upstairs with its sagging, foam-covered mattress. Beside the bed is a tottering tea-wagon piled with books to be read, and my old clock radio that only plays AM and whose knob for changing over to daylight savings is lost, so I have to use a pair of pliers on it twice a year.

I have been visiting married children with children, and the hum of the plane still makes me feel not quite myself. I think of how hard it was to get a good sleep in their guest beds—ones not saved for visitors, but thin-mattressed slabs for children who double-up, so I can sleep in solitary splendour. I still hear with a mother's ears—their little feet paddling down the hall and the soft whispers of their parents, as the cold-footed children scramble into bed with them.

I check my mail, reading everything but bills, look in the fridge, drag my bags upstairs and unpack. Now the laundry basket is full. I go to the store for milk, bread, apples and lettuce, unpack these items and thaw some chicken soup.

I'm at home in this small, quiet house, with pictures of my husband, parents, children as babies and as adults covering tables and walls, and grandchildren's photos concealing my fridge door. My books, my life are all here. I started writing in this home. Different memories—recent ones—some half-baked—of my life alone spew out of my computer.

When the time comes for me to leave this house, I'll be sadder than leaving my last home, where I enjoyed thirty-eight full years. I hope I shall give myself a talking-to and realize once more that there comes a time, when it's time. □

Life is simply one damn thing after another

—Elbert Hubbard (1856–1915).

TWO SEEN AS ONE

Two seen as one
his face
smiling and unforgettable
her face
dissolved into uncooked meringue
white, blobby, formless, smiling invisibleness

not *his* fault but the stranger's

When the *visible* disappeared
the *invisible* re-invented herself
into the sweet, firm-to-the-touch,
soft-centred, cooked meringue for presentation
on a large crystal platter to her new world

her
kitchen
was her studio

Her kitchen was her studio. She'd had thirteen of them since 1948.

STUDIO I was in Edmonton. A tiny, red and white one where she made ladies' delight pickle relish (after coming home from the glorious honeymoon in the mountains where she was sick in a pub from drinking beer and tomato juice, and her husband Hu had to vouch for her because she was under the drinking age at the time); baby formula (because breast feeding wasn't encouraged then, and she's regretted not doing so ever since); Thanksgiving turkey (and was hooked on that kind of smell, in their little house); hermit cookies (from her mother's recipe); and apple pie (made with directions from *The Joy of Cooking*).

STUDIO II was in Ottawa in a basement suite. A wringer washer and Tommy in a playpen crowded the small studio, where she made fried chicken in popover batter (from a recipe in the *Ladies' Home Journal*); Minute Rice (new on the market and served to guests as the *pièce de résistance*); and Pablum (from a round, blue box—good to store cookies in).

STUDIO III was at the university campus in Iowa. In the hot, muggy Quonset hut where their second son was conceived, her studio's two-burner hotplate and small icebox produced canned tomato soup, pancakes (Aunt Jemima mix), scrambled eggs (eggs fresh from the university farm) and potatoes, pork chops and salad.

STUDIO IV was back in her hometown, in a small house shared with another couple—her husband Hu was only home on weekends. The shared kitchen studio had a blue wooden toilet-training chair, where Tommy sat and ate raisins—Cheerios hadn't been invented yet. He didn't do what he was supposed to do, but waited until he was off the chair and his little training panties were pulled on again, in those pre-disposable diaper days. She made chopped baby food, Pablum and cocoa, and on the weekends they had roast chicken or beef (and she later had morning sickness and got a boil on her cheek probably from scrimping on weekend leftovers).

STUDIO V was at last in their own home. They'd planned it, and Hu helped build it. They had a new little boy, Bruce, and his carriage stayed in the doorway to the dining room, where the hum of the kitchen studio's Bendix washer processed its loads of diapers and kept him happy while he sucked his thumb (the only one of her six babies to do so). In this exciting new studio, with its dark green wallpaper patterned like chicken wire and hens and roosters strutting around the ceiling, she tried shrimp mull served on rice (her first sophisticated food, she thought, for one neighbourhood party); macaroni and cheese (pre-Kraft Dinner); real angel food cake (her mother showed her how to fold egg whites);

Sunday roast beef and Yorkshire pudding; and Sunday chicken with vegetables-in-the-pan.

Christmas dinners also flowed from this studio for thirty-seven years. They seemed not to separate, and she remembered the sameness of the menu: olives and celery and carrot sticks; sometimes shrimp cocktail; turkey, dressing and gravy; mashed potatoes; sweet potatoes and turnips; creamed onions with peas (Hu's favourite); tomato aspic (only adults liked it); pickles; cranberry sauce; and flaming Christmas pudding (again, only adults liked it, but the children adored Nanny's warm carmel sauce). Aunt Muriel, mentally slow, always came to visit, always overate and always threw up during the night. Aunt Ruby, a big-bosomed Buddha figure, wolfed her dinner. Aunt Pearl smiled and smiled—she'd been a teacher during the First World War and was an active member of the Women's Christian Temperance Union, so wine wasn't served. Other relatives and foreign university students sat at the table, which was damasked once-a-year. She would rather iron six white shirts than one of these tablecloths. And she remembered how babies would be taken from cribs, carriages or high-chairs and passed around from lap to lap, and they would put the coloured paper hats from Christmas crackers in their mouths and cry when they couldn't have what they reached for; in later years, when the children were adults, they could drink wine and lift their glasses in the toast, "Merry Christmas."

After a while, their first daughter, Jody, was born, and Jody grew to sit in the high-chair and spill her milk on the battleship green linoleum floor.

Then the first child, Tommy, died in a polio epidemic, and she lost interest in her studio and the whole house was sad. She made baked custard and red jello (because they slide down crying throats).

STUDIO VI was back in Iowa, at another Quonset hut. Its two-burner hot plate gave them pancakes, eggs (in all ways), soup and not very good stew (and she had morning sickness and ate soda crackers and caught a lot of mice because they were coming in from the cold).

STUDIO V. The home studio's wallpaper changed to white and grey with fat, red tomatoes next to jars and bottles of preserves. Another little girl, Lori, was born to crawl on the battleship green linoleum and pull herself up to standing at black and chrome kitchen chairs, and from this studio came oven-barbecued spareribs, real baked beans, wieners with bacon and cheese (a treat when Hu was away), apple pies and Christmas dinners (all this food consumed by larger numbers at the fully extended dining-room table).

STUDIO VII. Then a very small new studio was added at Hidden Bar Ranch. It was in a dull red trailer at the edge of a swampy poplar wood, where pink and blue harebells grew, kitty-corner from the horse corral and next to the single men's bunkhouse. By this time, little Jeff was born, and he slept in a portable cot and the other three slept in the back of the stationwagon. In this trailer studio with its ceiling so low that Hu had to bend over, she made Kraft Dinner with ketchup, salty Lipton's chicken noodle soup, peanut butter and banana sandwiches and Rice Krispie squares. Outside, a small, round Father's Day barbecue grilled hamburgers and steaks (from their own Angus cattle), and they went on picnics by wagon behind a team of horses—Nick and Flick—and had beans (in tins warmed on a fire) and wieners (cooked on sticks over a fire).

STUDIO V. Back in town, Jeff crawled on the battleship green linoleum and banged his head on the base of the round, black-painted oak table. She made peanut butter cookies, Christmas cake, shortbread, cranberry sauce, thimble cookies to be filled with raspberry jam, mince tarts and, of course, Christmas dinners. And another little boy, Danny, was born.

STUDIO VIII was back at the ranch, in a spiffed-up settler's cabin just for the summer, and Danny's four siblings slept in a real Stoney Indian teepee they had helped paint. She cooked in this newest studio for university students who worked for them for the summer. She gave them meat, fried potatoes, tomatoes and eggs for breakfast; packed lunches of meat, buns, hard-boiled eggs and fruit; and made dinners of stew, baked ham, ground beef patties, chili and pies. She also made chiffon cakes (the hens kept laying until she thought she couldn't make another of these cakes if you paid her); corn chowder and ham and cheese casseroles (for pony-club gymkanas and field days for friends); and homemade ice cream in a hand-cranked tub surrounded with ice plus salt (one sad day, the salt got in the peach ice cream, and you'd have thought it was the end of the world).

STUDIO V. Back at her city studio, Danny crawled on the green linoleum and pulled the telephone by its cord on top of his head, and she produced "souper burgers" (ground beef, onions and chicken gumbo soup); western scramble (ground beef with onion, eggs and shredded spinach and lots of ketchup); muffins and/or quiche for business associates (she prided herself in being ahead of many food trends); and Christmas dinners. At this time, her preserving kettle was sputtering, and her coldroom shelves held jars of crabapple jelly, watermelon-rind pickle, green tomato relish and pickled beets and carrots.

The wallpaper in the kitchen changed to an unusual yellow and white paisley. Bread, rising on top of the new dryer, was punched down by little Danny when he came home from morning kindergarten, and when the others came home from school, they had warm bread with honey, and she made the studio's third set of white organdy and pique curtains.

STUDIO IX. And then she had a small jiggling studio in a faded green trailer in southern Alberta at the Stampede Cattle Station, where she made gallons of coffee, ice cubes and beef sandwiches (for the men in cowboy boots who came to drink Scotch and buy or sell the purebred Angus cattle). Sometimes, at sale times, she cooked roasts for 150 people, for beef-in-a-bun, as well as bacon and pancakes (which were cooked on griddles on long barbecues in a windbreak next to the house, across the driveway from the sale barn).

STUDIO V. The wallpaper at their house back home changed again, to a fresh white, blue, green and red *mélange* of recipes, for such dishes as eggplant parmigiana and mussels marnier, neither of which the family liked, but she had to try them! The battleship green linoleum changed to subdued grey and white vinyl bricks, which showed every speck and drip.

Jody and Lori had, by this time, become her very efficient helpers in the studios. Bruce, Jeff and Danny, not unlike Hu, though he was competent in basic kitchen maneuvers, appeared to have little interest, except for the end results. The teenagers brought their friends to sit on the long, white benches at the studio table and ate and drank: peanut butter cookies, gingersnaps, Rice Krispie squares, homemade herb bread, baklava and gallons of herb tea. They laughed and they laughed and they laughed, and she hovered, though not over them, while she prepared dinners, knowing this stage wouldn't last long enough.

Of course, there were more Christmas dinners. During this period, she also had Christmas office parties for Hu's staff, as well as Christmas parties for faculty members (by now he was the Dean of Commerce). The studio's output for these parties was often beef-in-a-bun, with trimmings; ham-in-a-bun, with trimmings; and salads and sweets.

Before convocation, nervous young graduates came for brunch, where her studio produced muffins and fruit and scrambled eggs in her copper chafing dish. Many of these young people turned up in their lives years later.

Sometimes directors from Germany came for business dinners, and she made smoked salmon in endive, potato casserole, always Alberta beef, homemade herb bread, broiled tomatoes, steamed asparagus and chocolate mousse. The wine flowed, rose petals dropped, and she would once again empty the ashtrays, load the glasses, rinse the plates and silver, soak red wine stains off the table linen, and go to bed satisfied, though exhausted.

And usually, for Hu's December birthday dinner, when the children were older, she would make a big steak-and-kidney pie and invite a few friends over.

In STUDIO X, a great new studio back at Hidden Bar Ranch, in a big log house they all helped build, there was room for the whole family and friends to make lots of food:

- sandwiches of beef, ham or turkey (around a huge middle island, and she could watch a crackling fire, make dinner and see the children in the swimming pool, all at the same time)
- steaks (sizzled on two long barbecues between the dining room and pool)
- pancakes-and-bacon breakfasts (for high-school graduation parties)
- crêpe parties with choices of fillings, for sixty people (while the sun sparkled on the snow, their guests drank Bloody Marys and nearly everyone smoked).

STUDIO V. Back home around the dining-room table next to the studio, she offered gallons of coffee, cookies and mixed sandwiches to the smart young men and women who helped devise political campaigns and advertising strategies. She listened and even put in her two cents worth, and three out of five times, not counting nominating meetings, the end result was victory. And, of course, there were more Christmas dinners.

STUDIO XI was yet another studio, further west, at the Paradise Ranch in the interior of B.C., on a bay looking down to the end of Lake Okanagan. Ponderosa pines swayed by the window, or stood in perfect hot stillness, and she watched Canada geese honking past on their way to the apricot orchard down the lane.

Friends Mary and Jim, from Calgary, came every year. Mary helped make apricot chutney (whose pungent fragrance permeated walls and people) and pickled cherries (with gin and juniper), and the jars were boxed for shipment back to Edmonton in any cars going that way.

Large meals were made and served buffet-style from this glorious studio by the barefoot chef, wearing her chutney-stained apron, and every adult held a wine glass. The first grandchild came to visit, and everyone (except the grand-child) ate stuffed grape dolmades; homemade ice cream from a fancy Italian machine (sugarless, for Hu); leg o' lamb; ratatouille; yogurt with sunflower seeds, cucumber and basil; and corn on the cob (picked from the back garden and rushed to the pot, the way it should be).

STUDIO V. Back in the city studio, which was newly refurbished, with its last wallpaper, green and blue–tied herbs on a pristine white background, oak floors and an added greenhouse, they had toast, marmalade and tea, Welsh leek soup with parmesan cheese and salmon baked in foil with onion, dill and tomato. The humidity steamed the windows, and ice formed near orchids and sprouting bulbs, and the stars shone down at night and the moon lit the room where they drank wine and talked into the morning and felt a part of another world while they were safe in their own nest. There were to be five more Christmas dinners in this studio.

From this studio she hit her stride—party fare for over 100:

• JUST DESSERTS
lemon pecan bars
lemon pies
meringues

apple-filled phyllos
apple Calvados cakes
apple pies
pumpkin cakes (pumpkin-shaped)
blackberry and nesselrode mousses
baklava
chocolate pizza (in pizza boxes)
chocolate Cointreau cheesecakes
chocolate cherry cheesecakes
chocolate decadent tortes
cremè fraîche
fresh fruit salads
Stilton, cheddar, brie and crackers—before Martha
Stewart talked of such a way to treat guests

• MOSTLY WILD CHARCUTERIE
elk terrine
elk, bear and duck patés
rabbit compote
grape leaves stuffed with rice and elk
elk and moose sausage
romaine and elk strips, with nasturtium vinegar and
   basil oil
pesto pasta
wild mushrooms, with lemon and parsley
fennel olives
homemade mayo with basil
lime mustard
pepper jelly and apricot chutney
pickled cherries, with gin and juniper
herb bread, foccacia and onion and walnut bread
chocolate paté and wheatmeal biscuits

lemon curd and shortbread
Stilton and walnut torta and water wafers

• COUNTRY FARE
elk and city cousin paté
pork loin (with pear mustard)
plain Jane turkey, roasted, with wild plum and basil jelly
tiny wild rice pancakes, with red pepper jelly
homemade herb and onion breads
rye bread, with juniper butter
phyllos (filled with onion and apple puree or cheese and
    chutney)
stuffed grape dolmades
smoked trout rillettes (with marigold petals)
salad bar (banked vegetables, some raw, some steamed,
    and different dips, such as tapanade)
quark, with red pepper anchovy relish
quark, with basil pesto
cottage cheese, dill and yogurt
world's largest pecan pies (cooked in paella pans)
apple tarts
lemon curd for shortbread
old cheddar, grapes and crackers.
The studio was "really cooking" now. Later, she sold
some of these items—not that that was what she had
intended, but when asked if she would, she said, "Sure!"

STUDIO XI. She and her husband had their last two and
a half days together, part of the time at the studio on the lake,
by the vineyards in B.C., making tomato sandwiches (tomatoes bright red and warm from the garden) and picking strawberries (also bright red and warm from the garden).

No studio in the little motel in Langley, B.C., where they spent their last night. Next morning, her husband died in the saddle, riding in a cutting horse contest.

STUDIO V. She returned to her studio in the city and made flower arrangements from blue and white delphiniums, pink larkspurs, white mums, pink alstromaria, baby's breath and eucalyptus (in large, white baskets), for the church where her husband's memorial service was held. It was the only time she had cried while arranging flowers. From her studio, her friends catered the lunch for after the service.

STUDIO XI. She came back to the B.C. studio a month later, walked the hills and told herself, "That's it, I'll never see him here again," and she cooked applesauce (from early Spartans in the orchard and drank some wine).

STUDIO V. Returning to her city studio, she cooked for adult children, who wrapped up their father's businesses. She made pasta with pesto and barbecued hamburgers (and they sat around talking about how lucky they'd been to have had such a man as Hu in their lives).

She took turns with friends cooking gourmet dinners, and once had a Mardi Gras dinner from this studio.

She catered a daughter's wedding, adding a blue and white striped tent next to the greenhouse. One hundred and fifty people ate and drank:
- *paté a choux*, with red onion marmalade or cream cheese and red pepper jelly
- dried pears, with piped blue cheese, cornflowers and fresh herbs
- black olives, with lemon rind

- three salads (all in large clay garden pots)
  - rotini pasta salad, with basil pesto
  - curried chicken, melon and mint salad
  - barbecued beef salad
- vineyard paté, with fresh herbs
- rice and wheatberry melange
- French bread, with lemon thyme, tarragon or nasturtium butter
- apricot chutney, pepper jelly and pickled cherries
- wedding cakes (three-tiered, homemade carrot, with cream cheese icing, fresh violets and peony petal trim)
- fresh cherries (in a cutglass punchbowl with ice)

The wedding cake tilted, mock orange and peony blossoms dropped, the champagne flowed, three brothers toasted their sister, and life went on.

She wondered how many times she had sung "Happy Birthday" through the doorway to the dining room, and how many birthday candles were blown and how many wishes came true? She remembered their first child's last birthday with three- and four-year-old guests. The favours at the tables were big red suckers with Lifesaver faces, from Picardys. They were wrapped in cello, and the children thought they could melt this wrapping off by pouring chocolate milk over the candy. A party of Bruce's had little boys squirting ketchup and mustard at each other from new-on-the-market plastic bottles. She knew that her silent birthday wish was always the same: *I just want my family to be happy.*

STUDIO XII came after she sold STUDIO V with its greenhouse, and although it was almost as small as STUDIO I, of so long ago, she turned out many things all under the "Through the Grapevine" label, to be sold at craft fairs and a farmers' market (along with dried flower wreaths and arrangements):
- sweet and sour pepper jelly
- nasturtium-and-lemon thyme vinegars
- crabapple jelly and ginger jelly
- lemon curd
- tapanade
- biscotti
- French Market Soup mix

She also created fresh flower arrangements for weddings:
- brides' and bridesmaids' flower bouquets
- corsages and boutonnieres
- church flowers (Stargazer lilies, with their cerise centres and powerful perfume, too tight in bud, were bagged in plastic, and persuaded to open more quickly, next to her oven door).

Then it was back to STUDIO XI where she was denmother-cook for men from Washington who'd come to graft grape vines. When they came for dinner, they called "Hi, Mom—we're home," and they devoured

- pot roasts and baking powder biscuits
- baked ham and scalloped potatoes
- lasagne
- turkey and all the trimmings
- bacon and fried eggs, orange juice and raspberry jam
- pancakes and syrup and sausages
- apple pies and cakes
- bread pudding
- blueberry pie
- tuna salad, peanut butter and bananas in buns
- gallons of coffee, milk and ice cream.

Mornings, alone in her studio, she watched a beaver swim past each day, and she forced apricot and plum blossoms in wine decanters on her studio counters.

Later, at this same glorious studio, she managed and cooked for groups of writers and artists who stayed with her, for instruction and retreat, and the studio produced three main meals a day and coffee and tea breaks for up to fourteen guests at a time—another case of "hitting her stride":

- oatmeal porridge
- fresh fruit, with honey and yogurt
- whole grain homemade bread, with marmalade
- fresh valley apple juice and cranberry juice
- sautéed vegetables in tortillas
- vegetarian fourteen beans and lentils
- chicken breast stir-fries
- black bean dip and tapanade
- low-fat prune cake
- angel cake

- hot apple with lemon and almonds on low-fat ice cream
- low-fat quark, with pink pickled ginger
- lemon thyme pound cake
- de-caff coffee, herb tea and local wines

She'd thought, after reading a bed-and-breakfast novel, that she might have guests prowling the halls in the middle of the night, that there would be couplings or mysteries going on, but she saw no signs of such activity. One night she was so tired she almost didn't hear the bear's heavy breathing beside the bedroom windows.

Then fate changed what was supposed to be a yearly interlude, and STUDIO XI was no longer available.

Now in STUDIO XIII, a writer's studio in her crowded bedroom, filled with bed, books, family photographs, fax, PC and phone, memories change into stories about people and events, known and unknown. She goes into her head for thoughts never thought before, but now almost clear, in her new studio. She is a woman proud of what she has produced in her earlier studios—food, flower arrangements, bouquets.

Her first two published stories were about food. □

I got the blues thinking of the future, so I left off and made some marmalade. It's amazing how it cheers one up to shred oranges

—D.H. Lawrence (1885–1930).

The Bluebottle Fly

Thunk, *it went.* Thunk, zzz.

The huge bluebottle butted its way around the window edges on the west side of the glassed-in porch of the little pink-stuccoed bungalow where I spent my childhood.

My bed—a metal, cream and robin's-egg blue, youth-sized one—was moved from my back bedroom to the porch for the summer months. There were no blinds or drapes, so I was able to see the morning sky and especially summer storms that started in the west, fast darkening like a pulled-forward, black velvet hood on a crone's cape. Soft drum thunder would rumble, then the whip cracking would start and panes of glass under the bluebottle would rattle, and he would worry and thunk some more.

He was much too large and blue-black for me to get out of bed and hit him with my English funny paper or a pink slipper or my teddy bear. I knew he wouldn't hurt me. My mummy had said, "They have nasty germs on their feet and face, but they don't bite."

The thunder rolled louder than Uncle Rob's tummy, the lilac bushes scraped across the windows, the willow waved and dropped leaves, and lightning lit the room in flashes of bright light. The rain started hitting the windows and came in the one screened window at the bottom of my bed. My daddy rushed in and shut it after the wind had fluttered my bathrobe and blew my smelly jar, with its wax paper lid fastened with red elastic to keep the daddy-long-legs in it, off the window sill and under my bed, where I kept my "big-little book" collection all numbered like in a real library that I lent to kids and tried to collect overdue fines from.

The storm kept storming and the porch jiggled me to sleep. □

Fishing

I was happy, I think, in those days, trying my best to look and be older than I was. I didn't recognize that a good-looking candy-box needs to be filled with long-lasting jaw-breakers and that I would have to be terribly lucky to chart a bright future without searching the hills, valleys and streams for the right mate.

At that time, so long ago, few young women dreamed of futures with important careers. Most thought only of becoming a wife and mother and thought this position would give them a share of control in the marriage.

The *modus operandi* for successful hunting was to make the lure as alluring as a double-headed red geyser fly at the end of a fly-rod in a cold mountain stream. With a flick of the wrist, you would cast and the men would come, first one, then his friends and their friends, until one snapped and swallowed, and you'd reel him in. If you didn't like the look of his gills, you could throw him back and cast again. Maybe the next time with a blue-bottle whisker on a double-line sinker, you'd catch an interesting chap who'd strayed on his long journey from the ocean to the mountains beyond. He would be your prize catch and you would keep him—not to devour—but to turn into your Prince.

Maybe that's where the expression "poor fish" came from. □

An Audrey Story

My mother had a not-so-secret crush on Audrey Hepburn. Dad said it was harmless—she could have chosen worse—but I was embarrassed to tears when my friends came over after school and she was in her "Holly-Golightly-Breakfast-at-Tiffany's" persona. She would be smoking like a chimney, sitting on the window sill of the stair landing, singing "Moon River" and acting like she was my goofy sister instead of my mother.

Then she was the nun—pure, though without a wimple, and not getting angry even when our dog Daisy threw up. My dad could leave a beer bottle on the coffee table in front of the T.V., and she would just sigh, pick it up and place it gently in the top carton outside the back door for return.

Mother went in and out of Audrey as fast as a gopher pops up and down a hole. When she was out of Audrey, she was like any other normal mother barking orders, saying, "Do it *now*, not tomorrow"; "When I say no, I mean no"; and "Hurry up, you're going to miss your bus." But when she was in Audrey, nothing bothered her and she floated. The house was a bit of a mess, but we all smiled more—even me—and dad had a bounce in his step.

Sometimes she imitated Audrey running down the stairs to Fred Astaire's camera, calling "Take the picture, take the picture, take the picture," and he did and her glorious silk cape flowed like a billowing red slipstream behind her. Instead of a silk cape, my mother would take a white sheet off the clothesline and run down our sloping backyard through the asparagus bed to the lane, calling the same refrain, and the milkman in his truck smiled, tipped his cap and said, "Mornin' Miss Audrey, I've taken the picture—beautiful today in Paris, isn't it?" The whole town became part of her act. The whole town minus me.

My mother did have an Audrey Hepburn look about her: a bird-like frame and big eyes and teeth, but she didn't talk like Audrey—I'm sure she tried, because the inflection was similar. In a sweatsuit, which was what she generally wore, it was a bit hard to picture her in a brass lift with Cary Grant, like Audrey in *Charade*; besides, she never wore a hat. But she did wear short, white cotton gloves when she went out, which looked darned silly with her baggy sweats.

When she was Sabrina, back from Paris and living above the garage, mother danced around our patio, choosing between Humphrey Bogart and William Holden. She pulled apart daisies with, "He loves me, he loves me not," even though it wasn't in the movie script. I certainly couldn't invite a boy over when she was like that. Every so often my spine would tingle at the thought she might stay in Audrey and never come back out.

When Audrey was the princess with Gregory Peck and doing what the Romans do in Rome, my mother rode my bike like a scooter around the circle on our crescent, passing other bikes and rollerskaters, calling out, "Rome, Rome is my favourite city."

And when Audrey sang, "The rain in Spain is mainly on the plains" with that Cockney accent, my mother said, "C'mon Eliza, you can do it," and she would totter around the kitchen waving her apron with one hand and dropping daffodils around the long oak table with the other.

I was away at the Actor's Studio when dad phoned to say mother was unwell and would I come home? I'd been dreading this call for years.

He said what really tipped her over were the newsreels of an ageing Audrey: thinner than ever, hair starting to grey, as was mother's, age lines showing on her beautiful face, as they were on mother's, climbing out of a small plane in a hot African village, and then picking up a starving child, stroking his cheek, brushing off a fly and kissing him without ever a thought of a camera whirring next to her. My mother put Audrey on a higher pedestal than Joan of Arc, Marie Currie and Mother Teresa.

After Audrey's brief illness and death, my frail little mother couldn't stand it. Dad had to hospitalize her. She was now stable, and he wanted me with him.

As I walked the long corridor to where I could see she was sitting, the sunlight streamed through a window, lighting up those big wild eyes and that fetching grin. She seemed pleased to see me, although I'm not sure she knew I was her daughter. Towards the end of the visit I thought, *If it weren't for Audrey and my mother, what would I be like today?*

Just before we left, I told the nursing staff to let on to mother that she was at her home in Switzerland, that it was autumn, and that the grapes were ripening. As we walked down the hall, dad and I each holding one of her bony elbows, my dad said, "Audrey dear, let's go down to Lake Geneva and see the sun setting." She glowed that day like the real Audrey.

It was the last time I saw her, and if she thought my Dad was George, Fred, Cary, Humphrey, Bill, Rex or Gregory, so what? □

Nothing is wrong when done to music

—Jerome Kern (1885–1945).

how to

move a widow

I don't mean emotionally. I mean move as in moving van, from a house lived in for many years, to smaller quarters.

I wouldn't have believed it either, but honestly, I enjoyed moving after living in the same house for thirty-eight years, and you can too.

Pay attention, and I'll tell you what worked so very well for me. All you have to do is tailor my plan for your world.

I loved our house. We planned and built it when our eldest of six children was two years old. I didn't really want to sell it, but it was necessary for a variety of reasons. The memories are overwhelming—so much happened, mostly good, in that house. In the first place was the thrill of just having it, unfinished though it was. My husband Hu built the garage, helped the bricklayer and framed in the sliding doors. After that, we brought those darling, healthy, almost bald, blond babies home from the hospital.

Thirty-seven Christmas dinners were held in that house, and I don't know how many birthday parties, too. Children were ill, and our eldest, Tommy, at four and a half, was struck with polio, and he never returned to the white stucco, brown-timbered, shake-roofed house near the University of Alberta.

The kitchen was the heart of the house: babies under foot, a toy shelf, the telephone, sweet-smelling birthday

cakes, Christmas and Thanksgiving turkeys with sage dressings, homemade bread, onions frying for hamburgers or hot
dogs, Sunday roast beef or chicken, apple pies, lemon pies,
flapper pies, banana bread, peanut butter cookies, coffee-
bacon-and-pancakes and endless numbers of cups of tea.

We did many chores around that house: fixing, paint-
ing, enlarging, hanging wallpaper, scrubbing and moving
children's evergreen trees around the front yard like furniture.
Puppies were born in the garage, and kittens were born in a
clothes closet. Two small boys set two fires in the garage attic
club-room.

There was the excitement of organizing political
campaigns—Hu was a City of Edmonton alderman for two
terms and a member of Parliament for one four-year term. Of
course, these successful elections also had nominating campaigns, and then there were those other grim times when we
lost. (In case you hadn't guessed, it's more fun to win than
lose.) The old mahogany dining-room table saw and heard
heated discussions with family, friends and business associates and since the table has been sold, I'm glad it is incapable
of spilling what it has heard, although it could also tell tales
of laughter, love and family solidarity.

There were the first-day-of-school pictures taken every
year on the front steps and how the front door colour
changed from salmon pink to yellow to blue, all the parties
with friends, the one home christening, Hu's funeral reception, Lori's wedding and the surrounding friendly neighbours
who are still my friends. You know, you could write your own
version of this story.

Realize that the move to a new location, with some of
your possessions and all of your memories, will open up a
fresh and less complicated way of life. Consider this move as

just one more very natural progression in life, and if you're middle-aged or older, you will know you're mellowing.

The first thing I did after selling my house and finding new digs was to hire an antique appraiser. I sorted through silver (much of it rather black), china, glassware and old table linens, as well as furniture, paintings and sculpture. I spread it on every available surface and with a "count" on each set (e.g., one dozen, eight only) Mr. Cripps, my appraiser, gave me a detailed catalogue of all these articles. On his suggestion, I shipped a few pieces to an antique auction house in Vancouver, where they sold well. Then I tagged anything to be kept for my new place and things for each of the five children. The remainder would be for sale. I collected as many free cardboard boxes as I could, and I made three trips to a shipping supply store. You'll be surprised at how crumpled newspapers and "things" can fill so many boxes. It was about time I sorted this house—of course, I wondered why I hadn't done it all along. Perhaps you're more orderly than I am? For your sake, I hope so! Anyway, I loved seeing things I'd forgotten about. Many of these were destined for the garage sale or costume boxes for the grandchildren. I felt very virtuous throwing out some back-of-the-kitchen-cupboard items: old spices and herbs and gourmet food I'd been saving for about ten years, waiting for the right moment to dazzle. I began packing children's things and stuff for my new home with scads of newspapers I had hoarded and given to me by friends. I marked all boxes top, bottom and sides with big black print telling of each box's destination.

I took some of my oldest and better unwanted books to two book dealers and sold them. One dealer then came to the house and went away with a small truckload; the rest was boxed for each of the five children, my new home and the garage sale. At the same time, I told the children that any of their goods and chattels, including memorabilia, would go in the garage sale if they didn't pick them up. Those living out of town could make arrangements for storing stuff at a sibling's. It was up to them. Bruce still has numerous boxes belonging to Jeff in his garage.

I decided the dates of my garage sale and booked the ad in a local paper. I talked to two garage sale "junkie" friends who agreed to help me price my items.

Another dealer, recommended by the appraiser, came before I'd packed and made me an offer to take some items for consignment sale at his store but after my private sale with friends. These items were all sold within three months of my move.

I invited friends for coffee one morning amidst my initial packing mess—they could buy anything tagged for sale but had to sign up to work a shift at my three-day garage sale. I called anyone who had ever said, "Let me know if I can be of some help," and they enlisted, too.

The day before the garage sale began, a knowledgeable friend helped me set up on borrowed folding tables and card tables. Sticky tags with prices were affixed to most items, except some that were "bulk," and priced by marking on boxes "so much each."

When the sale was ready, the old garage was packed full, as was its driveway. I'd advertised "antiques" so when the serious shoppers for those appeared at the back garage, I took them separately into the house to make the sales, and they went out the front door. It worked well. Word-of-mouth had my large mahogany dining-room table and sideboard go to a daughter of friends, as did a large new hide-a-bed. I had wished one of my own children could have had that wonderful big table of my parents. Much had taken place around it through the years, but at that time, none of them had room for it, so away it went. Talking to oneself helps—just don't let anyone listen. Tell yourself, "Don't have regrets, just have memories."

Some of my children told me to "Sell everything you need to, but please just keep one or two nice things for each of us to have some day," and that's what I did. I now had a good list of my possessions, which was very useful for household contents insurance.

In my zeal to amalgamate my old world for smaller quarters, I made a few mistakes; I sold two mahogany dining-room chairs I should have kept. Now I have to borrow four, instead of two chairs, from daughter Jody when I have a sit-down dinner for more than eight.

After the sale, clothing not sold was taken by a young friend to the Salvation Army; the second-hand dealer took a load, and the other "clean-up" second-hand dealer took the rest, except for a few items put out with the garbage in the lane; overnight, scavengers removed those as well. Done, and there was money enough in my purse to help with some of my next home's needs.

I got three bids from recommended moving companies, took the lowest and was very satisfied.

The old living-room drapes were cleaned and taken to the drapery store to be re-cut for the new living room and one bedroom. The venetian blinds for the new place were ordered there, and new stair carpeting was ordered from another dealer. These window coverings were all arranged for installation a few days after I moved in.

Arrangements were made to clean the "old" house and spiff up the yard, after I moved out.

Moving day saw me "to-ing" and "fro-ing" with my car and stage-managing at the new place with the good-humoured movers. The boxes were piled to the ceiling, and it all felt very daunting to me.

I'd indicated furniture positions on a map for the movers and had each piece marked for room destination. The beds were assembled by them. The unpacking was slow but steady; I ate out for two nights. It was in the fall, and I could walk to a restaurant, which was good to get the feel of my new neighbourhood. I filed away kitchen stuff so we could move around in that small room, and I hung the pictures everywhere because the furniture was in place. Do this picture-hanging step as soon as possible—it'll make you feel you're home. Then I only had to unpack the china, glassware, books and personal things. I had to buy three new bookshelves and had two more made.

My daughter Jody painted the kitchen walls, and I had padded built-in benches and a table made for the kitchen. This furniture proved to be a great idea. It cost a bit more than I wanted to spend, but it's turned out to be money well spent. Don't you love it when a small extravagance turns out that way?

My happy story is, instead of a house much larger than I needed, with upkeep problems, I now have a smaller place and pay a monthly fee. I've even taken a turn as condo secretary, so now I know my neighbours better and have learned a lot. I like the feeling of being more "urban," nearer to more people, and within easy walking distance of eleven book stores. Large boulevard elm trees shade my patio and provide fall perfume, leaf crackle and homes for birds.

I still have my memories of our old home—a nice young family live in it now—and am contentedly building memories of my new life in my new little home.

Planning a Move
(Tailor this list to your own needs.)
1. Sell house, find new condo or apartment, set moving date based on possession date of old house.
2. Make appointment with appraiser for furniture, artworks, silver, china, crystal, linens.
3. Sort through above. Label what you're keeping, giving away or selling, so this stuff can all be marked in your catalogue. Tell children they're responsible for any boxes marked with their names.
4. Make appointment with the first of second-hand dealers.
5. Make appointments with new homeowner, to take measurements for drapery, blind and carpet dealers.
6. Get newspapers from friends and boxes from stores and shipping supply company (address in Yellow Pages).
7. Get bids from three moving companies (get references and check).
8. Sort books—some to book stores but also try to get a dealer to come to your home.
9. Set pre-sale and garage-sale dates, place ad in newspaper and invite guests to pre-sale.
10. Arrange for cleaner for old house and yard-work help after vacating and before new owners move in.
11. Arrange insurance on new house and contents.

12. Notify any companies necessary with change-of-address. Send change-of-address cards to Christmas card list friends and give house purchaser your new address forwarding labels.
13. Advertise any appliances for sale.
14. Phone second-hand "clean-up" dealer to come after last garage sale.
15. Sell some furniture to house buyer, if possible, and re-tag.
16. Attend a few garage sales in area and/or get experienced person to agree to help price and set up your sale.
17. Set up, including pricing articles for sale. Have supply of bags and boxes.
18. Hold garage sale.
19. Clean out freezers and give contents to family and friends.
20. Moving day.
21. Clean empty house, check yard and turn over all keys to new owner. □

MESSAGE FROM MY MUSE

Now my dear it's *coming*

but can't you dig deeper?

You say perhaps you're only two inches deep

while others are a foot.

Do you really believe that?

Just write every day

and you'll be surprised.

Just as already, fragments are appearing

from crevasses

unsuspected

and they're

deep

deep

deep

though not enough sunlight reaches them

and that's what you want, isn't it?

Have you decided yet if you want to

write to make *you* feel good

or your reader or both?

You say both.

Well then, go ahead.

First, start dredging for grains of sand.

They may itch and irritate
but then
they'll pile up big enough
to fill a pink plastic teacup
and you'll have lines enough to fill a fish poacher.

Then you'll dig some more and the pages will fill and
spill on the floor and go out the door and down the steps and
around the corner and down the road and to the publisher's,
who will smile and want
"More please"
and send you a cheque
and tell you to pack your bags
"You're going on tour."

Tommy

A little boy of almost four and a half. Getting a cold, perhaps, but tonight is Hallowe'en. We'll let him go out with his younger brother. Baby Jody is too young to go.

My mother made the clown suits. One's still in the costume box. We took pictures of the two little clowns.

Next morning, there they all were: Tommy and Brucie in Jody's crib, all trading licks of suckers.

That night Tommy cried—he was so sick. Doctors told us that flu symptoms, especially pain when lowering the head to chest, must be watched.

My husband out of town.

Doctor at the house. "Yes, it's polio."

My parents with us. Hu back home.

I sleep in the room with Tommy. He's quiet and looks puzzled. For six days we nurse him at home. On the sixth night he breathes too hard. Nanny and Gramp babysit the others. We take him to the hospital. Quarantine, so we had to leave him. Went home to bed.

Middle of the night, doorbell. Our doctor, who is a friend, in tears. "We lost him."

My first thoughts: Poor little boy, we weren't even with him. *Then:* What about Bruce and Jody? Hu has had enough sadness—his father, his mother, his friends—I've only had sunshine.

My first tragedy—at twenty-five. □

So Much for Cyrano

I've been reading the classified personal columns since Mrs. Broeksma, my landlady, got me hooked.

We both saw it in Thursday's paper, and we knew it was our Hank. With the girl's name of Roxanne, I thought it might be some sort of "take" on Cyrano de Bergerac, but no, it has to be quiet, pathetic Hank, the young man who lives in the basement suite.

Where are you Roxanne Channing? I've wanted you for 23 years. In our 1972 school photo you sat in front of me, Hank. We are destined for each other. I need your heart in my life. Please write.

Pathetic, isn't it? I've been living here for four years and he's been here for three, and I still haven't said much more than "Good morning," and he only says, "Good morning" back. The age is about right, poor guy.

I'll bet Roxanne was a blond perfect type—one of those girls the world smiles at. She was probably just nice to Hank, he read too much into it, blew it up and permanently fell for her. I'm dark and scowly. The world didn't smile on me, so I don't attract even the Hanks of this world.

There's something sweet about him, though: soft spoken (when he talks), medium height, thin, reddish-blond hair, and weathered skin on his hands and face, except for his forehead (it's quite white from wearing a cap at his job). He works at the zoo, and I figure he probably talks animal-talk better than people-talk. Once when we had skunks under the back porch, he lured them into the ravine without anyone being squirted.

In the spring, when it was green in sunpockets before anywhere else, the ravine's music would waken him in the morning. He'd see tiny animals investigating *his* lair, and he'd watch the runners in Spandex with their Walkmans and waterbottles, and wonder if Roxanne could possibly be one of them—so close but still a dream.

Roxanne possibly has a career, a marriage and babies, and she is probably just stepping down as president of the Junior League, or she is the incoming chairperson of the Breast Cancer Fundraiser Gala, or both. If only I could save him from the sadness of finding she's beyond his yearnings. What would happen if someone asked her if she's Roxanne?

Maybe Mrs. Broeksma understands him better than I do. She said, "Poor boy. He's clean. I'm Dutch—if he can please me, he's O.K. He doesn't smoke, drink or have women in his room. Pays his rent on time and shovels the snow. He's a good boy. If he finds a good woman, I'll be sorry to see him go."

She was even mean enough to suggest to me, "And what makes *you* so smart that you think you know what Roxanne's like? Maybe she's a shy young woman who'd think a steady, clean-living boy like Hank would be a prince? You say his ad is pathetic? Well, maybe *she* has a secret longing for *him*." □

the first
time

The first time I drank too much is hard to remember because, well, I drank too much. I know I was at the Jasper Park Lodge. It was a cool August night, the moon was full, the stars twinkled disapprovingly, and there was a boy from Quebec who was a waiter. My brown and yellow waitress uniform hung limply at Cabin L, where my roommates lay on their beds, wondering where I was.

There were blankets and beer and a fire, and the boy and I were not alone. We sang and maybe I sang in French, although I wasn't bilingual. I don't remember much else, except a wrestling match.

I left and stumble-floated through the pine forest, so different from the poplar woods back home.

It was the first time I had gone to bed feeling I was sliding on a moving globe, floating dizzily—too discombobulated to undress, too topsy-turvey to tango, too tipsy to titillate, too tight to talk. My roommates would have to hear about it after work, which would start in four hours.

Pity I can't remember more, though perhaps not. Sometimes blocked memories can be a good thing. □

One reason not to drink is so you'll know when you're having a good time

—Anon.

A Lemon Lover Remembers

Pay no attention to the idiomatic uses of the word "lemon," including a "sourpuss" and a "car that's defective," but think of the lemon's long history in our world and in our lives. Lemons were first grown by ancient Greeks, then Romans. The Moors planted lemon orchards in Spain in the eighth century, and in the sixteenth century Spaniards introduced them to the New World. By the eighteenth century, lemons were almost as popular in Europe as tulip bulbs, and conservatories called "orangaries" were built in France and Britain to contain these most glorious of tree fruits. Near the end of that century, Spanish missions in California were planted with lemon, orange, olive, pomegranate and fig trees. In individuals' personal histories, the lemon's sour citrus flavour is so often connected with specific memories that one taste of its sharp flavour will cause an event to immediately flood into our minds.

Can you remember the lemonade stands of your childhood? In years past, the stand was set on a wooden apple box, small cheese glasses awaited the buyers, real fresh-squeezed lemon juice was mixed with sugar and water, ice was chipped from a block delivered to your mother's ice box from a horse-drawn wagon and, finally, the cool nectar was poured from a big white enamel pitcher with a chipped, dark blue rim. Now, lemonade stands are set in plastic toy wagons, tippy throw-away foam cups are used, and either neon-coloured Kool-Aid or a frozen pink lump is mixed with water. Ice cubes from the fridge are added, and the cool concoction is poured from plastic juice containers with flip-top lids. Then, and now, more product was consumed by the stand's proprietors than customers, and no one got rich—it was just something to do on a summer day when you were very young.

Hot lemonade made with real lemon juice had to have honey, not sugar, as its sweetener and was a mother's medicine for colds severe enough to keep children home from school. I remember drinking it after being allowed to get out of bed, sniffling and coughing, wrapped in a pink wool blanket in front of the fire, while a howling blizzard blew crazily around our little home. Now, powdered lemon drinks, in packages and containing sleep-inducing medicine, come from the drugstore to help children recover.

A happy ending for an old-fashioned Sunday dinner in my childhood home used to be lemon meringue pie—my mother had a light touch with pastry—made with lard in those days before cholesterol was feared. The pale brown, flaky crust held a clear, satin-smooth, puckery lemon filling on which the beige-tipped cloud of meringue balanced before I squelched it against the roof of my mouth, melting it into a sweet-sour lemon memory.

My grandmother made lemon curd to go in tiny tart shells. I ate them with two bites, though the soft, sensuous substance squirted all over, and I would then eat the second one whole. Lemon curd is very easily made (see p. 110). Now I spoon it on packaged gingersnaps.

Good lemon squares—the ultimate in sweet and sour, addictive confections—are sprinkled with powdered sugar and eaten at any time of the day or night. There are never enough lemon squares (see recipe, p.109).

On a cold winter day, a thin slice of fresh lemon is a great addition to a cup of hot tea drunk in front of an open fire or at the kitchen table. Iced tea, on a hot summer day, made from well-prepared, strong tea and poured into tall glasses half-filled with ice, added sugar, a wedge of lemon and a fresh mint leaf is a perfect summer beverage for sitting on the back porch.

An icy martini, with its glass rim wiped with lemon zest and a twist of zest in its clear depths, is a sophisticated, time-honoured tongue-loosener. A tall, frosted glass of gin and tonic with a wedge of lemon is the drink to swill at a summer barbecue.

A most versatile herb is lemon thyme—my favourite of all herbs. I pick it from pots on my patio, my fingers squeezing the lovely lemonness, and wonder if I'll get my pound-cakes made with it for the freezer. I paper-bag some of this herb to dry from a hook above my kitchen table, and I use it fresh, in gazpacho, salads, roast chicken and every summer pasta dish. I wonder why I didn't plant a field of it and just forget about basil. Lemon balm is another favourite herb. Its handsome, mint-like, dark green leaves give off a thick lemony scent mixed with the beautiful fragrance of the tomato plants towering above. I chiffonade the balm leaves into fruit salads, or I chop finely for including in poundcakes and muffins.

A whole cut-up lemon with onions, in the cavity of a chicken, not only flavours the roasting bird, but is a most welcoming perfume in my home. Sprinkle lemon juice on fish, clams, oysters, caviar, avocado, bananas, cantaloupe and salads, and you will find that the lemon enhances the foods' flavours. If you've squeezed too much lemon juice, freeze it; it's much better than bottled juice. A slice of lemon in ordinary tap water makes it more palatable. Get a zester—a small utensil that quickly shreds zest off your lemon rind in longish threads. Squeeze lemon in broccoli and asparagus cooking water, and they'll stay green. Squeeze lemon in the cooking water of cauliflower or rice, and they'll be whiter.

Lemon lovers rejoice: as yet there are no dire health warnings against using lemons in our food.

The Recipes

Lemon Squares:
Crust:
1 c. flour
1/2 c. butter
1/4 c. sugar
Blend well and press into unbuttered 9"x9" pan and bake at 350° F for 20 minutes.

Filling:
1 c. sugar
2 tbsp. flour
1/4 tsp. baking powder
the juice of 1 lemon (3 tbsp.) and lemon zest
2 beaten eggs
Mix well and pour over bottom layer. Bake at 350° F for 25 minutes and sprinkle with icing sugar and cut when cool.

Lemon Curd

3 large eggs, plus 1 egg yolk
1 c. granulated sugar
1/4 lb. unsalted butter, cut into pieces
finely grated rind of 2 large lemons
6 tbsp. fresh lemon juice

Put eggs and yolk in the top of a double boiler. Add the sugar and whisk lightly to mix. Add butter, rind and juice. Place over hot water, moderate heat. Cook, un-covered, stirring frequently with a rubber spatula, for 20 to 25 minutes or until the mixture is as thick as heavy cream sauce. Strain. Put into tart shells.

Lemon curd freezes very well. □

*A goldfish has a memory span
of three seconds*

—Anon.

Evening in Paris

When my mother was going out for tea or at night with my dad, she smelled differently than she did everyday. Going out came from that dark blue bottle (not Milk of Magnesia, but Evening in Paris), and she only used it for special occasions.

It sat on the middle, lower part of her vanity table, because it would have been knocked off one of the higher sides where the mirrors were hinged. I could put my face right up to the centre, stationary one and almost close the other two behind my head, tilting them to see three of me: profile, back and sides. When I did that, I could talk to myself about injustices and what I would do if only I had a baby brother or sister.

I thought the bottle was the most beautiful thing in my parents' bedroom. Much prettier than the French ivory hand mirror, the nail buffer with its greyed suede and the tortoise shell comb that slid through my curly hair after it had been first tackled with the pig-bristled black brush. My mother sat me on the cane-bottomed dresser stool, with a "Don't wiggle, dear. Sit still."

"But you're pulling," I'd cry and finally she would be finished.

Sometimes my mother would dot her Evening in Paris pointer finger on my nose, after she'd touched her own skin behind her ears and her wrist, and I would be able to smell her after she had gone out.

In later years, Lily of the Valley, in a small, thin bottle, was kept in her purse. Then, even later, when she was as old as I am now, Elizabeth Arden's Blue Grass became her scent.

I once was in the south of France and bought some single essence perfumes: lilac, violet, lily of the valley and rose. I loved to hold the small, gold, black-labelled flacons and sniff the pure essence of my favourite flowers, but when I wore these fragrances my husband hated each and every one. Why? His favourite perfume was Joy, a glorious mixture of roses and I don't know what else.

My mother loved lavender. As a child, I hated it. She had it in little, mauve, see-through bags in the linen closet and in her underwear and silk stocking drawers. The tiny, dried, grey flowers would sometimes escape, and I thought they looked like sad insects or faded, tiny mouse droppings. She also used Lavendomeal in the bath—hers, not mine. These crystals were kept in a round, wooden container and were sprinkled with a flat wooden spoon into water that whooshed from the fat tap. They made the bathwater milky and lavender-scented. Lavender and oatmeal—how English can you get? □

Minds are like parachutes
—they only function when open

—Anon.

COMPOSITION FOR KEITH

In the middle of the night

the man next door

played an ebony grand piano

half the size of his living room

music I had never heard before

and the lilacs under our bedroom window

sent musical perfume

perfumed music

scented soft sounds of

mauve and purple and heliotrope

ruffling and hanging

then floating

in air.

When lilacs bloom

perfume essence reappears

fluffy blossoms play chords and trills

and I think of him

his perfumed songs

still singing.

Magazine Tracking

I think books and magazines—as well as human contact, T.V. and radio—must influence one's speech patterns. My periodical choices have certainly changed through my life. As a child I gobbled British funny papers. The only two names I can recall are "Crackers" and "Jingles." I think they tied in with the Girl's or Boy's Own Annuals, which appeared at Christmas. The North American funny papers and big-little-books were filled with Maggie and Jiggs, Blondie, Dick Tracy and L'il Abner, amongst others. After that I don't remember what I read until *Seventeen*, a new magazine, appeared when I was less than seventeen. I devoured it. I also read *Downbeat*, a jazz magazine. Married at nineteen, I began to find *Good Housekeeping* and the *Ladies' Home Journal* very necessary. I had been modelling since I was fifteen and now began reading *Vogue*, *Mademoiselle*, *Glamour* and *Harper's Bazaar*. Mother and dad gave us *The New Yorker*, and I read whatever articles appealed: "Talk of the Town," columns on fashion and theatre and always M.F.K. Fisher and James Thurber—I hooted at his cartoons. I didn't know then that M.F.K. was a woman. I've now read, I think, most of what she wrote. I remember the *Saturday Evening Post* only for its Norman Rockwell covers, *Life Magazine* for its photos and later *Family Circle* for its gentle humour. By this time, the children were older, and our mailbox was crowded with *Newsweek*, *National Geographic*, *Aberdeen Angus News*, *Quarter Horse Journal*, *Chatelaine*, *Saturday Night*, *Maclean's* and the *Economist*.

As the children left home, my magazine needs changed again, and I drifted towards upscale food and interior design publications. Some of these show flower trends, and I still want to be up-to-the-minute for my occasional flower-arranging jobs. Now I also read *Vanity Fair*, *Canadian Living*, *House and Garden*, *Harrowsmith*, *Martha Stewart Living* and *Victoria* (not to be confused with the catalogue *Victoria's Secret*). My more recent interest in writing is demonstrated by the piles of *Other Voices*, *Grain*, *Prairie Fire* and the *Globe and Mail's* Saturday book section scattered around my home. Sometimes, I splurge on the *Sunday New York Times* for its book reviews.

Of course, my tastes have changed, as I've changed. I'm not sure if I'm really going backwards or forwards with my tastes. Because of all this reading, I have to sort magazines frequently and catalogues almost monthly. But they have their uses. The papers go to Jody for her puppy training. When the shelves are too full, I extract Christmas issues, for decorating and food ideas, and the remainder go to Value Village. □

The time to repair the roof
is when the sun is shining

—Anon.

it all worked

out for the best

I know I was a disappointment. My mother had, with great difficulty and a small monthly payment, subscribed to an education policy to come due when I had graduated from high school. I would then sail forth onto the sea of higher learning at the university on our doorstep.

I think my dad was surprised at mother's tenacity in this wish for my future success. Although she never told me (there was much she never told me) that an education is terribly important for a woman, I think she realized that I shouldn't have to depend on a husband. In the back of her mind she was thinking of an older sister, who had been widowed with two babies. This sister's husband had been a pensionless high school principal, and she had no particular job prospects. My mother wisely absorbed Marjorie's plight, and in her long-headed way tried to provide for her small daughter's safe future. Remember, I was born in 1928, on the cusp of the Depression.

That small daughter sailed through her days, a grasshopper while most of her friends were ants. No wonder my mother was often dismayed when I showed few signs of striving for excellence in school. I was content to glide.

A confrontation came when I was working in the summer as a waitress at the Jasper Park Lodge. Mother phoned to say I'd failed my high school algebra and Latin exams and must return to Edmonton to study and write the supplemental exams, or I would not have university entrance. I refused, and my fate was sealed.

Two years later, after I had fallen in love with and married a man I think both parents were surprised I'd captured—he was working on his fourth degree, was teaching at the university and was so nice—she produced the $1000 education fund to help us buy our first house.

My parents had not owned their own home until I was a teenager. □

dollhouse

It was so big, when I sat on its roof, I could see out my bedroom window and spy on whomever was coming or going at the Beckers' back door right across the lane from me.

The secret of being a bore is to tell everything

—Voltaire (1694–1778).

Daddy had ordered a dollhouse for me one Christmas. Knowing nothing about such matters, he probably didn't ask mummy's advice and must have thought, "the bigger the better," so I ended up with a dollhouse that took up about an eighth of my tiny bedroom in our small bungalow in the university area of Edmonton.

I rarely played with it, though mummy had valiantly made colourful little hooked rugs for it and had painted small watercolour pictures for its walls. There were even a few small tables and chairs.

I don't recall, over sixty years later, what little dolls I may have used, probably paper dolls, or what make-believe games I thought up or with whom I played.

I only remember sitting on the dollhouse's rough green roof and how the cream-coloured chimney stuck up at the end next to my wobbly bookcase and how Mr. Becker came home at the same time every night but my daddy didn't. □

My Mother Told Me

When I was about ten, a man not my father fell in love with my mother. She said she had to tell someone and that person was me.

When I think back, I'm not surprised. Hadn't people been saying all my life, "Ethel's so beautiful, the child looks just like her father." I couldn't tell then, but from pictures I've seen since, she was glorious: curly dark hair, huge brown eyes (I think they were limpid), graceful body, beautiful smile, soft voice. She was everything men liked in those long-ago days.

Mother was more unsettled than I'd ever seen her. She was pacing around the kitchen, wiping the spotless counter tops, repositioning the flop-down toaster and the blue and white striped cookie jar filled with puffy sour cream and raisin cookies, refolding the hand-embroidered tea towels, refilling the dog's water-dish, and putting fresh water in the small, cracked bowl of soaking sweet-pea seeds.

She wasn't wringing her hands, but I felt as though she was. She said, "What have I done? But I didn't do anything—how could that man have thought I'd be glad? I can't stand it—your dad would be so hurt. He'll think—oh-what-will-he-think—that I'd led him on? Don't you breathe a word of this to anyone, not till your dying day."

I guess I couldn't wait. □

THE CUCKOO CLOCK AT AUNT MAUD'S

Please hold me up
so I can see the little bird
cuckooing at me.
Did she know we were coming?
Is she hot in there?
Does she have water?
Where is her mother?
Can she sing other songs
when we come to visit?

I know she's waiting.
Will she fly away some day
and sit on a telephone wire
and tell the world what time it is?
But maybe she won't want to leave her pretty house.
Maybe she'll want to stay and see Santa Claus
and children's birthday parties
and us coming to visit
and new puppies and kittens
and the hummingbirds
at the windowbox filled with nasturtiums
and my aunts and uncles playing poker
and Uncle Lester coming home from the hospital
when he's fixed the sick people
and does she pop out of her house
when it's nighttime and dark
and only the moon and owls are awake?

Oh, I wish I could take her
and her beautiful house home to our house
and she could cuckoo to my friends
and my dog and my mummy and daddy
and I would take good care of her
till we bring her to visit you next summer.

what mothers

don't know

Now he tells me. About thirty years after
the fact. I don't remember it, although he does. He claims that
I always insisted he should get some fresh air and exercise
before dinner on cold and still winter days.

According to him, I sent him down the dark back lane,
around the corner and across the street to the skating rink for
an hour before our six o'clock dinner, dressed in snow-pants,
tassel-scarf and a woollen toque, with his scuffed skates and

their knotted, yellow laces draped over his shoulders and his mittened hands holding the rustless blades.

He says now that he hated skating—the noisy jostling in the boys' change room, the shoving and taunting on the rink and his fear of embarrassment. He recalls no exhilaration from the crisp air; no euphoria from gliding like the wind or skating backward; no pride at stopping quickly at the boards with ice chips flying; and finally no excitement from the girls' teasing cries of "Catch me, Danny." Poor little guy.

With my "Have fun, dear—be home by six" ringing in his ears, this seven-year-old would grudgingly leave the house. Why didn't I know? He walked as slowly as possible to the turn near the lane's end, while checking overflowing garbage tins for interesting trash and spotting rabbit tracks, dog pooh deposits and yellow pee cavities that made interesting snow formations for him to examine.

Then he would leave his skates at the Cox's gate, walk up their perfectly swept back sidewalk, ring the bell, and be invited in for warm cookies, hot chocolate and a visit with a mother whose son was the "Terror of the Skating Rink"—a whirling, stick-handling tease of a boy. Our quiet son would talk philosophically to this adult who claims she always enjoyed his visits but had no idea his mother thought he was at the rink.

Sure enough, at six, Danny would appear home for dinner—slightly pink-cheeked from the cold. My response to his boot thumping while he dislodged snow, flung his skates to the lino and sniffed loudly a couple of times, was "Oh, you look *so* bright and healthy—you must have had fun. Wasn't it *lovely* to get out skating? You must be starved. Everyone's home. I'm just going to put out the dinner, dear. Get washed up and come right to the table."

And he would. □

The Wedding

It was the wedding from hell for us, but it didn't start out that way.

I was working as a florist for our town's most exclusive and expensive wedding planner, Gerald DeBath of Sissinghurst-Spry. He designed whole weddings—the backdrops, flowers at the club, flowers for the wedding party and suggested musicians. He even had a hand in helping choose the menu, though he did leave the bridal dresses to someone else.

I was just a lowly helper, not allowed to do bridesmaid or brides' bouquets but only table centres, corsages, boutonnieres, flower girls' head garlands, baskets and table and cake decorations. I have to hand it to him—Gerald—he did have exquisitely subtle taste. He wouldn't make a living in Hollywood though, from what I've seen of some of those weddings. You'd think since so many of them are repeat performances with different players, the bride would choose "low key," but oh no, the bigger the gardenias, roses, trailing smilax, ivy and orchids, the better. Talk about size, and they must be heavy too! Whoever gets hit with one of these bouquets flying through the air could be knocked off her feet. And the bridal gowns were so beaded, sequined, puffed and poofed, you'd think they were going to be featured on a float in the Rosebowl Parade. A purple banner stretched across the brides' chests with "Queen of Poof 2000" would be all that was needed.

It was summer and I'd been doing bows—hundreds of them for corsages to be used at the next five weddings. My fingers were aching from twisting wire, and I tuned out the other helpers—Jean, John, Mary and Kim, who were whipping up pew markers of gold salal, sunflowers and meadow grasses with creamy raffia bows, for the big country wedding tomorrow. They were up to their knees in flower stems and leaves. Anyway, I was closest to the corner of the shop that

Gerald called the "consult corner." While I couldn't see the two people talking, I could catch most of their conversation.

Either the bride had a very soft voice, or she just didn't get to say much. The bride's mother said, "What about red roses with baby's breath—so old-fashioned, don't you think, and what I carried at my wedding."

Gerald, that sly old diplomat, said, "Yes, they are lovely, but don't you think they would be more appropriate for a Valentine wedding?"

I knew he hated cliches.

"How about an autumn theme? After all," and he actually broke into song, "*la-de-da-de-da-de-dum, 'tis autumn.*" Then, in his best Sissinghurst-Spry fashion, he rambled on. "Oh, I can just see it. We'll have everything in fall tones, but of course a little lighter: peach lilies, apricot roses, maroon and rust alstromaria, variegated ivy and for zap, we'll introduce just bits of chartreuse with French mini-mums, orchids, hypericum berries and trailing miniature maple leaves. And we'll do willow branch archways at the entrance and behind the head table—you do want a head table, don't you?"

"Of course," the bride's mother replied.

"How would things work if you didn't have a head table?" the bride piped up.

"It's usually for smaller weddings than yours, my dear. Four hundred is a large number of guests." I could tell he was grinning from ear to ear. A wedding for 400 would help the old balance sheet. "Now, have I got this? One bride's bouquet, five bridesmaids', two flowergirl's head wreaths and baskets, a ring-bearer's velvet cushion, boutonnieres for the groom, five groomsmen, two fathers and two grandfathers and ten corsages—we'll get the dress colours later for these, church flowers, pew markers, car decoration—we don't very often do this, but just a velvet bow and some branches of maple I think—then the club decorations: russet velvet tieslips over the chair backs and russet cord on the topiaries, and I think we should have a lighting consultant, and I know just the one. I've worked with him heaps of times, and you'll be amazed at what a difference good lighting has on an event. Here Sandra, you take these disks I have from the best musicians in town. Pick who you and your fiancé like the best, and I'll book them. You can also list any special selections you want. Mrs. Correlli, I'll fax you a proposal, and closer to the wedding date we'll firm up the particulars. How's that?"

And he skillfully ushered them out of the shop before they knew what had hit them.

And so, the summer months passed. More weddings under the bridge, or down the aisle. Anyway, it was the day before the "*la-de-da-de-da-de-dum 'tis-autumn*" extravaganza, and Gerald had a crew building archways of birch trees. Their leaves had been "whiffed" with rust, gold and red, because we hadn't had Indian summer yet, and they hadn't turned color the way he wanted them. Then waterpics with peach roses and lilies were wired onto the branches, along with scads of rust and chartreuse hypericum berries. The arches reminded me of Kenneth Turner's work I'd seen in Gerald's floral arranging books—parties done for the rich and famous in London and New York. So why couldn't we have the same thing right here in Saskatoon?

I knew the bride's father had money, but no one seemed to know what he did. Over the topiary trees we were making for the table centrepieces, Kim and I speculated he was a slum landlord in Toronto, or the silent partner in a waste disposal company, or the money behind two boy-wonder software geniuses. He was going to get mighty big bills from this party. Lucky he only had one daughter.

The bride drifted in and said, "I love what you're doing, can't I see the bridal party flowers?"

Gerald explained, "Oh no, they're done the morning of the wedding, so we can get them to you at their absolute peak of perfection. And I'm going to personally bring them to your house tomorrow. One o'clock—O.K.?"

I love it when the bride herself checks in. Not many of them do. More often it's those perfectionist mothers.

Next day, known as "the day of," Mary, Gerald's oldest and most trusted florist, and Gerald, himself, did the bridal party bouquets. Subtle floating creations they were. Jean was assigned the job of individually wiring and taping each flower, leaf and bud so the creators could assemble the soft petaled apricot roses, double white freesia, tiny chartreuse mini-mum buds, rust cream alstomaria, hypericum berries, variegated ivy and a bit of springerai fern. This bouquet was wired, instead of being in a holder with water-soaked foam. The bride's bouquet was tied with white, double satin ribbon, and the bridesmaids' with apricot. Their dresses were russet velvet. Swatches of the gowns were stapled to the work sheet on the wall over Gerald's work table.

Kim and I made the flower-girls' head wreaths of cluster roses in peach and white, with hypericum berries and ivy. As well, we did small baskets for them to carry filled with alstomaria and roses trailing russet and creme silk cording. We bagged extra of these flowers labelled "Pin on velvet ring pillow." Then we did all the corsages according to the list Gerald gave us—and there were many!

Gerald finished the huge fake stone urns filled with four-foot branches of mini-maple leaves and crab apples, white spider mums, rust, orange and peach gerbers, lilies, roses and curly willow. John made all the church pew markers. All of these were loaded in our dark green van with Sissinghurst-Spry in gold Old English script on the side and zoomed to the church, later to be repositioned at the club.

A reliable seamstress who did the velvet chair covers was installing them after a scheduled club lunch.

Gerald said he would personally deliver the wedding flowers to the bride's home three hours before the event, so pictures could be taken with them. We all waved good-bye, some had a smoke and some their fourth coffee, though they drank it standing, instead of sitting. (That's Gerald's rule: "No sitting down on the job around here" and since he never does, we can't.)

Half an hour later, Gerald was back with all the bridal party bouquets looking like thunder and shouting, "They hate them."

"NO, what's wrong with them?" we all cried in unison.

"Too small—not splashy enough—subtle's not in their vocabulary, so get wiring and taping, all of you. Thank God, we've got flowers left. They want big? We'll give them big, they won't be able to see over the top of them. Sure, put some maple leaves in. Give them more lilies, add some spider mums, trail on some more ivy, give them the works. We've got one hour to do it and get to the church."

I could hardly bear to look at Gerald, though when I did, I saw his face looked like he'd been sprayed with the flower mister—beads of sweat dribbled from his face into the bride's bouquet. I wondered if that would bring her good or bad luck or would just develop into brown spots on the rose petals.

The van had just returned from the first delivery so we loaded it for the trip back to the church, while Gerald changed into a clean white shirt and slacks. He told me to follow. I could help pin corsages and boutonnieres. "There's no telling where this crew is likely to put them." So I followed, at least I thought I was following, but somewhere there's another dark green van in Saskatoon like ours and I ended up at a packing plant instead of the church. Knowing it was too late for me to go to the church, I went to the club, decorated the cake table and waited for Gerald's wrath to catch up to me.

When he finally came, I helped him position the pew flowers on the clubhouse railings, in the washrooms and on the bandstand, and removed broken blossoms from the large urns. I thought he'd be furious still, but instead, he'd turned giddy.

"The bride's mother got into our well-marked corsage boxes and gave them to the men. Then she put two boutonnieres on some guests, which left some with none. I tell you, I've never seen anything like it. So I had to go down the aisles and exchange corsages for boutonnieres and I never did find the groom's special one so I took a rose out of an urn and pinned it on him, wished him good luck, the poor bugger. He'll need it marrying into that family."

The next morning when I dragged into work, Gerald was on the phone laughing like crazy and saying, "You've got to be kidding. I don't *believe* it!"

When he hung up he told us a friend who'd been a wedding guest had reported on the wedding. He said at the reception, when the toasts were well under way, a friend of the bride's family had toasted the mother of the bride, saying "We know how much you're going to miss your only child—your masterpiece—you'll need something else to care for," and then presented her with a white rat, cowering in the corner of a black wire cage. The mother tearfully thanked him. Her husband looked stunned. There was silence. Then all the guests lifted their glasses and roared, "To the mother of the bride!" □

A rose is a rose is a rose

—Gertrude Stein (1874–1946).

grandmother
spends part of a day at the lake

We've eaten toasted bagels with peanut butter and grape jelly.

We've played badminton, taking turns with the sun in our eyes.

We've played battleship, with the older brother giving unwanted hints to the others; his advice isn't appreciated. The day stretches long, and it's just past eleven.

The children are pink already—a bad UVB day. Grease them with No. 30 sunblock. Now it's time for water sports. I put life jackets on the under six-year-olds. The nine-year-old boy, the only boy, spends twenty-five minutes blowing up a raft, and now he's dizzy. On the sand, four little girls chase the Canada Geese away. Hope the geese take their lice with them!

The raft deflates, because it has a hole. (To say it is time to go would be an understatement.)

After their swimming, the four girls, including the two-year-old, get in a warm bath. Giggling and splashing ensues.

The boy pouts and says the holiday is no fun—he needs a friend. He's allowed to drive the car through the cherry orchard and smiles at last, but it's just a brief interlude.

At lunchtime, the girls and even the boy all laugh, eat ham and lettuce or peanut butter sandwiches and pickles, and don't spill their milk.

It's amazing how food in children's tummies relaxes them. They wiggle and poke, then stretch out on pillows on the floor, watching *Anne of Green Gables* in the fan-cooled house, and I relax. I've made it through part of the day at the lake. □

Elephants can't jump.
Every other mammal can
—Anon.

I Don't Much Like

There are some things that I don't much like.

I don't much like it when people say, "What was your name?" Do they want my maiden name, or do they think I had another name in another life?

I don't much like the little plastic things on bread bags. I like twist-ties instead.

I don't much like it when a tiny grandchild shouts at me with a red face, "You're not the boss," and my sense of humour fails to activate immediately.

I don't much like it when I occasionally realize that I haven't stayed in the same physical shape my mother did.

I don't much like the way I'm off and running on a new project before I've completely finished the first one. These "lap-overs" are hard on me and my little overflowing house.

I don't much like the thought that while my mother's words are coming out of my mouth, my daughters are not heeding this great wisdom—just as I didn't.

When people ask me to do favours or to volunteer or to arrange flowers, I don't much like to say "No." I'm afraid I won't be asked again.

I don't much like when a grown-up child chastises me for still trying to "mother" them. Have I started to resemble a mom on a sitcom?

I don't much like feeling guilty when trying to evenly distribute my "quality time" with my fourteen grandchildren. Some of my own children, daughters-in-law and sons-in-law suggest that I don't spend much time with all of them because

I'm doing too many other things. I tell myself that many others have managed to balance their lives satisfactorily, so I should be able to as well.

I don't much like feeling guilty when I do anything *but* clean the house or tidy my desks. I've continued a "clipping service" I performed for my late husband, and now I send clippings to my five children; I fear they seldom heed these gems of wisdom or the latest in scientific discoveries for their problems. These clippings pile up, and although I'm not knee deep at the moment, it has been known to happen.

I don't much like being told by family members that I don't have very good under-the-sink garbage-pail etiquette, or that I don't fill tea cups full enough. One of my sons claims that I have no concept of "the bag is full," which I admit to, but how do I explain that the opposite happens when I pour tea? All I can say in my defence is that I have erratic depth perception. The pouring problem also stems from trying to keep young children safe from spilled hot tea. I did have six children, after all. Regardless, another son occasionally reminds me that he's forty-eight and can now handle a full cup of tea safely.

To me, purposely ignoring the full garbage pail shows that I like to live dangerously and am too busy to empty it. □

*You can't make a soufflé
rise twice*

—Anon.

shepherd's *pie*

August 26, 1996

Hu dear, ten years ago today you died in front of me

with no warning. I didn't get to say good-bye until after the wild ambulance ride, when you were lying on a gurney at a hospital in a strange town with a white sheet over you.

Shock was a wonderful thing for me, slowing and dulling my reaction. I remember phoning our cousin Dorothy and telling her. She got Bob out of a meeting at the University of British Columbia, so he could come and take me to Vancouver. A stranger, whose name I never found out, took me to the motel to pack our things and check out. I forged your name on your credit card.

I remember phoning our daughter Jody and telling her that you had died and that you hadn't suffered. Your death was immediate—a massive heart attack while you were still in the saddle on your horse, Twister. You always said you wanted to die with your boots on. You got your wish, didn't you? I told Jody to tell Bruce, Lori, Jeff and Danny that their dad was dead.

I still can hardly believe it happened. Bruce and Lori came to Vancouver to meet me. Someone made arrangements to fly your body home to Edmonton.

I was so used to your being away on business, I had to keep telling myself you wouldn't be back. But I kept thinking about you: your quiet laughter; your deceptively slow, long-legged walk, as you came towards me; the way the skin on your arms, where there was no hair, was fairer and smoother than any of our babies'; the shape of your feet, like Jeff's; your strong and competent hands, with the shortened tendon on the palm; the way you could talk or argue so effectively; your glowing smile when you leaned over to kiss me after the birth of each of our six children; how solid you felt when we hugged or danced—nothing spindly about you (your body, your whole being, was solid but never dull); your boyish enthusiasm when you had a new idea and your energy and laughter when you were successful; your thoughtful and beautiful love-making—better through the years; and the way you talked poetry to me. Although I didn't write the poems down, their theme is in my heart.

Months after you died, I think I was still stunned. My brain secretly whirled around, saying *You don't have a choice, you don't have a choice…accept this. You were very lucky to have been married to Hu.* My weight dropped to under 120 pounds. I felt as though I was eating enough, though my throat kept tightening and I was uncomfortable swallowing. I remembered the same thing happening when our first-born, little Tommy, died. I've learned to always bring soft foods to people who are crying.

I remember when I was a very young child going to the Princess Theatre with my parents. If something scary or sad came on the screen, daddy would hold his fedora hat in front of my face and say, "It's only a movie." He couldn't bear to see me or any other children cry. Remember, when my dad would go for a walk immediately after one of our children began howling from a tumble, perhaps off the back of the green chesterfield? Dad's "It's only a movie" must have stayed in my head; I couldn't react to what was before my eyes, even though I knew it was real.

When I was invited to dinner with a group of our friends, my arms and legs felt heavy—as though I was swimming in thick cake batter. *Did it show?* I wondered. I knew I was smiling and was amazed that I was laughing too, because at the same time I was thinking, *You should be here.*

Our friends have been more thoughtful than I think we ever were to new widows. I knew my women friends would rally around—many of those friends were married to men with heart conditions and would have been thinking, *It was more likely to have been my man.* They took me to lunch and phoned to see how I was getting along. They said they couldn't believe how I was accepting your death. I knew I had no choice, and I felt that if I could act upbeat in public, somehow I would be all right. Besides, if I fell to pieces, how would that help the children?

Ah, the children. My dear, there have been many heartaches with our five since you went away. I will have to reach you in some other more private, cosmic way to tell you in detail what has gone on. One serious health problem—no, not a recurrence of Bruce's cancer, but Lori has MS, and there has been one more divorce. And much, much more. But I'm fine. I tell them that I hope things will have improved by the time of my memorial service, and they assure me this progress is most likely, because I've said I intend to be a *very* old, mellow woman some day.

We now have fourteen healthy grandchildren—you'd love all of them. I see or talk to our family every week, though more often to Jody, Lori and Danny than Bruce or Jeff. I think they are all secretly relieved that I'm living an independent life, though they have been helping me financially. Remember how we used to joke when they were growing up, and the bills were flooding in, "Oh well, you children can look after *us* in our old age"?

Since you left, I've kept busy doing flowers for weddings, parties and large functions, much as I used to do. Whenever I use white freesias, I think of our long dining-room table (that once was mother and dad's, which I had to sell) and all the faces down either side of it and the freesias placed in the middle. Other flowers also cause a flood of memories. Paperwhite narcissus—remember their strong perfume, and how each fall I had bulbs of these flowers in French mustard pots at the back of the fridge? They were in competition for space with the few—you said more than a few—mouldy leftovers I didn't immediately throw away. I thought I was being thrifty! Remember how I planted paperwhites around the house, for a great and glorious show at our big pre-Christmas parties? Now I give bulbs of these flowers to local grandchildren and have only a few for my kitchen table. I used to preserve borage flowers, remember? You considered this herb a weed, because it grew alongside the driveway. But remember, too, toasting Jody's twenty-first birthday at Hidden Bar Ranch with champagne? Those starry blue blossoms bounced on the bubbles and turned bright pink. I haven't used borage since you died. In our old house, nasturtiums used to be on the patio behind the living room, and they trailed down to that hidden cellar door entry; I always bottled the darker blooms with spices in vinegar and put silk nasturtiums around the bottle necks. I'm still doing that, but now the fresh flowers come from Jody's back lane.

I moved two years after you died, and after Lori and Randy were married in our living room. We had a party for 150 wedding guests with a blue and white striped tent over the greenhouse patio. I knew I couldn't stay in Windsor Park, so I sold our house (by word of mouth). Where did I go? Well, I knew there were eight condos in a secret pocket of South Garneau. I had a lawyer search the titles, and then I wrote to the owners, and finally one told me, "Anything's for sale for a price." After much free advice from some of our real-estate friends, I dealt alone and bought this man's condo. Strangely, I had a good move. It was about time—thirty-eight years—and our house did need sorting. I've squished much of our stuff into this small place, south of where I grew up. There's a comfort factor in living in a familiar area, where young people roam the streets, though there are still plenty of seniors around, too. I can walk to the university, a seniors' centre, grocery store, drug stores and the wonderful Old Strathcona area, and I feel safe.

I've had a physicist from England visit me every year for a few weeks, while he collaborates with a colleague at the university. He's a friend of Helen's, and he and his wife, who's also visited me, have become my friends. The children, especially the boys, tease me about this physicist visitor. They say they can imagine me, a non-mathematically gifted person, sitting across the breakfast table from John, who is explaining quantum physics, and me saying, "Oh, isn't that fascinating," just as though I understood every word.

Before I moved from our home, Lori stayed with me for the year Danny was in England for school, and then Danny stayed. He moved with me to my new digs but now lives nearby. An Iranian graduate student is my boarder these days. He seems to be knowledgeable about many things medical, though he's had me steaming my head with oregano this week for my cold, and so far the herb treatment doesn't seem to have cured me.

For three years, each time for longer periods, I ran artists' and writers' retreats out at the vineyards in B.C. It was the most satisfying job I've had since being a full-time mother to our kids and a helpmate to you. You know, I've always enjoyed praise; you were always generous that way, and I have received heaps from my guests. I did brochures and advertised widely, with the best results from the travel plans' column in *The Globe and Mail*. I ran some sessions without a visiting artist, and at others that great painter and raconteur, Toni Onley, flew in for a few days each session. Mary Dawe held the writers' retreats. I fed and slept up to fourteen people each session at the vineyard. That meant three "squares" a day, plus coffee and tea breaks. Each session I held one big dinner around the old table transplanted from Hidden Bar Ranch. (That table summons a whole other set of memories, doesn't it?)

I invited local artists and writers to join the men and women who came from across Canada, and I had a truly interesting mix at these retreats. I'd read a book about a bed-and-breakfast and had visions of people creeping the halls in the middle of the night with all sorts of intrigue and coupling taking place. Perhaps I slept too soundly downstairs (our bedroom was taken by paying guests), but I saw little evidence of these activities. I hadn't been as tired at bedtime since we had colicky babies. A guest later confessed there *had* been a story right under my nose, or rather, above my nose. I guess I was too pre-occupied with my proprietor tasks to notice. I know sometimes when I was in the kitchen, darn it, I'd miss what guests were laughing about. I made money though.

One spring, I cooked at the vineyard for a team of six men who were up from Washington to graft new varieties of grapes onto our old rootstocks. You'd be delighted with this turn of events—you always said it didn't make sense for the wineries to want us to only plant for volume and that some vinifera would be planted eventually. These men were young and had to be fed in a manner like you said your mother had fed thrashing crews in the thirties. My menus were different from the writer-artists'—no herb tea, yogurt or chicken breasts for them; it was pot roasts, hams, scalloped potatoes, carrot cakes and ice cream. I kept a journal of this time, including menus. In it, I told stories of the nights when the ants took over the kitchen and when the water line was frozen. Dear, why didn't I keep a journal of our eventful life together?

This year I've had many calls from people wanting to come to my retreats, but I've had to retire, gracefully I think, since Jeff and Noni have moved to the big house. They're in family practice in Penticton and have four children. Jeff has been helping manage the vineyards. This ending seemed the best for all.

I'm still selling some food products, as well as dried and silk flower arrangements. I sometimes teach flower arranging, occasionally do work for a construction company in its show homes and still work sporadically for Alli, at Design Plus. I've stopped selling my wares at craft fairs and the local farmers' market, though I did that for six years. Besides that, I've found a new occupation—writing. You must be surprised. I think how easy writing seemed for you. You dictated speeches to me, and I would take them down in my own version of short-hand, while we travelled in the car, and then you could give the speech with just your few notes on a single card.

I can't do anything like that, but writing about memories is a lot like writing letters: just write what you're thinking, and what's on the page will sometimes surprise you. My memory for some details is faulty, but for some weirder, other details, I think it is faultless. Remember how I could never argue logically and how annoyed you'd be when I would say, "Never mind logic, I just *feel* that way"? This trait of mine either drives our sons mad and they scold me, or they roll their eyes and humour me, which I prefer. I've also started to write fiction, and I'm having trouble being the observer of imagined lives. It's odd; blobs of realness will spurt out sometimes and I think, *Where did that come from*?

One of the best things about writing—not the quietness of it, nor the satisfied feeling you get when a line or phrase flicks out in exactly the right way—is belonging to a writers' circle and hearing of other people's struggles, and how they write of these struggles, often twisting their truths into beautiful stories that I appreciate. Perhaps if I'd had a life as a psychiatrist and had "heard it all," I wouldn't be so struck by this new existence; I've made new friends who know as much about me through my pages of writing as do some old friends.

Before you died, I'd never thought of being a widow, and now I think I'm a recovered widow—whatever that means. I'm now older, nearly five years older, than you were when you died at sixty-four. My proverb is "Nothing stays the same in life, it gets better, or it gets worse, or it just gets different."

I think of the things that returned in style: long skirts and short skirts, straight hair and curly hair, dark lipstick and light lipstick, hats and no hats, pale skin and tanned skin, big bosoms and little bosoms, bad manners and good manners, roast turkey and turkey sandwiches, bread and bread pudding, little cars and big cars, egg whites and angel food cake and roast beef and shepherd's pie. I think of coming from a good marriage to a good widowhood as one big shepherd's pie: eat it too fast and you get indigestion; cook it too long, and it'll dry up and toughen. The old ingredient is memory, programmed into your soul, and the new ingredients are new experiences. The gravy for the pie is good happenstance, and the topping is what you orchestrate yourself.

Happiness can come around again.

What do you think, dear? Aren't you glad for me? □

Age can't protect you from love. But love, to some extent, can protect you from age

—Anon.

Some Days

Some days, Mother, some days, I wish I had taken your advice. Learn those skills you said. "Bridge and golf, bridge and golf, bridge and golf"—I know what pleasure they brought you.

I remember the card parties, where bridge was played on those folding card tables, which were stored behind the big chair in the living room. The tables were topped with green felt, and your chintz, yellow and brown table covers, which were edged in brown bias binding, went over the table corners. Little candy dishes were filled with licorice allsorts, and you served non-alcoholic drinks of ginger ale with rhubarb juice. Card players wrote on the little pads and tally cards with tiny pencils. Male guests smoked cigars and cigarettes. Then you had a lunch, and it was sandwiches of asparagus rolls with white bread, shrimp salad on white, gherkin pickles, stuffed olives and real angel food cake with pink icing. Tea was served with lemon. The men, wearing dark suits with vests, laughed so loud. The women, wearing flowing and flowery dresses with their hair in waves or rolls, giggled. They all were thin. Everyone was then, though I don't know why.

I can remember it more clearly than a party in my own home twenty years later, though that could probably be thirty years ago.

It's like I have total recall, mother, for fragments of my life as a child but only angora fuzziness for the many days and nights I spent with Hu and your grandchildren.

I can see the men and women sitting in our living room. They're laughing, the fire is crackling, a nylon leg is crossed and a shoe slips off a heel. A drink of Scotch is spilled, and a wife runs to the kitchen for a tea towel. She is on her hands and knees blotting, blotting, while the husband keeps talking and is handed a fresh drink. I can't see the faces or hear what we were talking about, but the scene repeats and repeats. □

*If I'd known how old
I was going to be, I'd have taken
better care of myself*

—Anon.

STROLL OF POETS AT THE UPPER CRUST CAFE

Slippery sidewalks,
ice fog hovers under lamp posts.
Tuesday, seven o'clock
at the Upper Crust Cafe
brown beetle coffee bean floats on
soft-foamed de-cafe latté.
Paper-laced biscotti
waits dunking.
Faux marble table by friend Shelly
holds this scrawl.

Four poets spout their words
to be inhaled
by lamp-lit room.
Perhaps at lunch tomorrow
words will spurt from carrot soup,
tabouli and quiche of the day.

Am I *crazy*?
Can *I* do this two weeks from now?
Can I invite wine and coffee sippers,
poets and friends
into *my* head?
My innermost head?
My brain?

Shall I let each cadence fall
like lead, feathers, perfume or succulent slivers?
Will I sweat each word
with narrowed breaths?

Will they understand
will they understand too well
will they say "I've been there"?
or will youth so wise
think old bones not cool?

Who cares,
are my poems for me or them?

I will speak new dreams and old.
Some waft in waves
some hide in cells
and tear
like tape from skin.

*Let me listen to me
and not to them*

—Gertrude Stein (1874–1946).

footprints *on the wall*

Forty-nine years ago my water broke at a friend's home and labour began for our second child's birth. There was a spring snowstorm that year, and we'd been thinking of early calves dropping and hoped we wouldn't lose any.

I had vaguely remembered my first confinement in 1949 when I was twenty, when new mothers were not coached and pep-talked. Now in 1951, at almost twenty-three, I again remembered my first labour: "Mrs. Harries, don't roll on your side," and then I gulped the sweet-smelling gas, and oblivion came before the episiotomy pricks.

This time I gave a good-bye kiss to husband Hu and soon after...where was the doctor? The nurses wouldn't believe me when I said the birth was near. My words were ignored, especially by the cold-eyed one. She may have been competent, but God—those eyes—she was heartless.

She said, "Slow down, you're not having the baby yet," but I knew better and told her so. Still insisting I was wrong, she said, "Wait. The doctor's on his way."

Perhaps I panicked—stiffened up and made things worse. I started to push.

"Don't you dare do that—cross her legs, phone again."

I didn't dream it, and the wind howled, and the small stucco hospital rattled, and I rattled and maybe I howled, though I'd been told only Italian mothers did that. The howling resembled the sound cows make—a groaning, moaning, mooing, panting, urgent effort of sounds like no other. Still the nurses waited. But in spite of them, the baby came—a boy, the smallest of all our six.

I'd been put to bed in the second month and given pills so I didn't lose him; at age thirty-one, he had testicular cancer and maybe the pills I took were bad ones and caused this disease. The doctor whose records, thirty-one years later, were destroyed, said, "Were they small white ones?"—as if I could remember such a thing. And he told me, "They would be either DES or something else—don't worry, the Canadian prescribed dosage was smaller than the States." We'll never know if the pills caused this grief. In my anguish I wasn't going to start a Canadian class-action suit. I just wanted to know "Why?"

This doctor's name was on the hospital's certificate of birth—the one where the baby's tiny feet were pressed onto a black ink pad, then carefully touched on a square above the time and date of birth, under the child's name and place of birth. (Those tiny prints, toes like dots. It's funny to think of those toes now in size twelve Reebocks running marathons.) Every night as I climb the stairs to bed, I pass, hanging on the wall, the six sets of footprints.

If there is a fire I will rescue these prints under glass and the smiling picture of my children's father. It is the smallest pair of prints that trigger the memory of that night—a snow-storm, cold eyes, panic and instead of joy, relief. □

*Don't let yesterday use up
too much of today*

—Will Rogers (1879–1935).

The Cherries Are Ripe

In the last week the cherries in the orchard turned from a pale unripe shade to the colour of a fine old claret. It is early in the morning, and a noisy helicopter flies overhead. It blows droplets of water off the cherries at their stem ends—the fruit will not split as it swells under the increasingly hot sun but will be perfect.

A handsome grey-haired grandmother wearing a sari sits watching over three little boys, who are dangling cherries from their ears. Their piercing laughter floats down the orchard rows, as they collapse in the long grass, their T-shirts, lips and teeth purple-stained with cherry nectar. They see how far they can blow the cherry stones and gleefully shout when they hit a target.

Two graceful young women and three strong young men climb the three-legged picking ladders and disappear into the leafy branches overhead. There is a plunking sound as the cherries start to land in their buckets. The men gather and pile the shining marbles into boxes and load the truck, while the women keep picking, the sound muffled as the buckets fill.

When the back of the battered blue truck is loaded with cherry boxes, the grandmother and boys and the cherry pickers leave. Only the birds remain, pecking at the puffy, red beads. The birds' trilling and chirping alert the bears, who will trundle down the mountain tonight, just before dusk, and have their cherry feast.

The Recipes

The best way to eat *fresh* cherries, that is if you can't pick them fresh and eat them then and there in the shade of the cherry tree, is to pile them in a huge bowl of melting ice in the middle of a picnic table. With your friends on either side of the table, have a contest of who can blow the pits, or click them between the teeth, the furthest. Be sure to wear dark clothes.

Pickled Cherries with Gin and Juniper

Cut the stems short (about 1/4") on 2 lb of cherries—either sweet or sour. Pack in jars.

Bring to a boil, and simmer 10 minutes:
4 1/2 c. white vinegar
1 lb mixed white sugar and brown sugar
6 cloves
6 lightly crushed juniper berries
1 thinly cut peel of a lemon
2" stick of cinnamon

Add 1 c. gin to the mixture. Cover and let steep overnight.

The next morning strain over cherries, making sure all fruit is submerged. Store in dark.

Serve as a Mediterranean hors d'oeuvre, alongside olives, marinated mushrooms and anchovie tapanade. □

WATER

Her raised face
with eyes closed
met the stinging drops
they pierced her pores
and travelled through
and down her body
softening tingling
moistening even her brain
she thought and laughed aloud
not for her, someone else's music
or words in the shower
and her thoughts were good
warm like the water that nourished them
and the pelting pellets
drove her to other places
and she thought aloud of a black prairie sky
its jaws spitting briefly, then torrentially
and a muddy dug-out
with soggy, black cattle
scrambling up its clay banks
to trundle to the safe long windbreak
the rancher had left
and she thought of him
in his long, yellow slicker
the rain sluicing off his cowboy hat
onto the horse's neck and rump
and the difference between the gumbo up north
and the sandy southern land
under that endless sky
she had known so long ago.

The Ten Dollar Bet

By this point in our cross-country trip, we'd reached South Carolina, and I was dozing off and on while Judy took her turn behind the wheel. She's a good driver. As a passenger, I can sleep through most anything, though on this particular drive I always stirred when we moved from the slipstream of a large transport truck into the left lane. There was that different, whistling sound and the air pressure changed.

We'd speculated that afternoon about the men who choose to drive those big vehicles. They were no different, I supposed, from the men in charge of a plane or train—different degrees of training, responsibility, culpability and financial rewards. Certainly, there were different degrees of respectability. With trucks, we knew there would be a kind of pecking order; probably the bigger, more chrome-laden carriers that transported the most exotic loads were at the top of this order. Though in the Northwest, we'd see huge cattle-liners, loaded with their snorting, dripping cargo, and decided they'd be a big payload. We'd also noticed at truck-stops that no driver looked "fit." If he didn't have a beer belly hanging over his large, silver-buckled belt, he had a number of other detractions—face full of stubble, narrow eyes, sharp-tongued, yellow fingers from heavy smoking, greasy hair. In short, no one you'd want your daughter to marry.

The slight swaying of the car, and that distinctive wind-whistle sound of being next to yet another tractor trailer, made me glance up from my slumped position at the side of a moving, white billboard. It announced "Carl's Coffins, Bed Your Loved Ones in Comfort for Their Last Sleep." It was a catchy slogan, and I thought *I wonder if cremation's not popular in this state?* When we came even with the cab, an unexpected apparition grinned down at me but only momentarily, because Judy didn't relish side-by-side tête-à-têtes with one of these behemoths for long. The driver's face was painted white with clown-like black eyes and high, raised brows. He had a wicked grin with white fangs and something black, a hood perhaps, on his head. Startled, I wondered if I'd dreamed it, but decided it had been for real. Of course, attentive driver that she is, Judy hadn't seen him, but acknowledged passing the white truck.

We tried to guess a reason for the driver's appearance— either the coffin company required this garb for their drivers, which seemed highly unlikely and a bit sick, or he was testing a costume he'd wear at a local Beaux Arts Ball, also highly unlikely. Maybe the long, lonely hours on the road had driven him mad, and he'd stopped at a local Malabars and turned himself into who he really wanted to be. *Or* he was on his way to meet his wife in the next town, where they were destined to take first prize in the scariest couple contest at their church's annual Fall Box Social, or his sister was a Hollywood costume designer and he would wear her creations. Whatever.

If we didn't get too far ahead of him, our paths might meet at a truck stop and we could find out. Judy bet me ten dollars we hadn't guessed the correct reason yet.

It was approaching midnight when we came to a likely looking motel-gas station. No sign of the white coffin transport, but we were tired and checked in. I asked the man at the front desk if he'd seen or knew of Carl's coffin truck; he turned white and said, "Guess you aren't from these parts. Two years ago we had one Hell of a wreck down on old Crooked Creek bridge. Carl's coffins were piled like split kindlin' on both sides and down to the river. Damn fool driver—drunk as a *coot* on his way to scare his ex-wife on the night she got back from her honeymoon with old man Carlson—lost it at that curve before the bridge. Last year, this time other drivers saw the ghost, too."

I shivered and gave Judy the ten I owed her, and we went to our room. But we both had a hard time falling asleep. □

*People who know it all
can be dangerous*

—Anon.

WHERE ARE YOU?

Do you exist,

that link between

what was and is?

Are you in another soul

re-worked

abridged

reduced

but not lessened.

Is your essence

living in another form?

I have only changed

by growing up

and seeing our children suffer

and would I suit

your secret soul

or would my

sensibilities,

sharpened since you left,

be too strange for you

to tolerate and love once more?

mother

Occasionally in some mirrors or shop windows, when I look sideways, I see not me but you. How can that be when you left sixteen years ago, bright-eyed, though speechless and helpless, in the university hospital? So why have you re-appeared in mirrors, glass and glances? Twice when I visited your youngest sister—she's now older at eighty-three than you were when you died—she cut a perfect quiche with your deliberate motions. Her laugh wasn't the same, but your face, your quiet voice and your wise perceptions were there for me to see and hear.

I wonder, will I appear in mirrors, glass and glances to my daughters? Surely not to my sons; they don't have the look (or the hair for that matter). And then for my daughter's daughters, will their great-grandmother flicker at them through new-age mirrors and glass? Perhaps by then she will step through the mirror and tell them of her trip from England when she was seven and had five sisters and how every second one was blond, blue-eyed and fair skinned, while the others were dark haired, brown-eyed and dark skinned? My mother and two sisters carried the dark French Huguenot genes; the other three who knows? □

Time, which changes people, does not alter the image we have retained of them

—Marcel Proust (1871–1922).

The Year We Had Hens
at Hidden Bar Ranch

(A Memory Elicited by a Plain White Hen's Egg)

One year, when our five children were young, we decided a thrifty thing to do would be to have some laying hens at our ranch near Edmonton. I looked forward to all the cakes there would be in the freezer—chiffon cakes made with corn oil were in vogue at that time—and the children thought gathering eggs daily would be a lot of fun. However, despite good intentions, the best laid plans often go awry.

Chickens are not like dogs—they don't do as they're told. These particular hens took to pecking their own eggs. Beth, a young student helper we had that summer for child control, suggested that we take some of the broken eggs, fill them with a mustard mixture, and put them back in the nests to more or less teach the misbehaving hens a lesson. Either that ploy or something else cured them of their erratic behaviour, and soon I had so many eggs that I was pleading with the old dears to "Stop. Please stop."

We had so many eggs that we were increasing our neighbours' and relatives' cholesterol levels, so when fall came, we had Harold, the fine man who worked for us, slaughter all the henhouse inhabitants. Then we had an unforgettable session of bagging chicken parts for the freezer.

Chicken fricassee, chicken soup, chicken casserole, chicken and dumplings.... We had a chicken in every pot, and it wasn't long before the children were pleading for hamburgers. □

*It's impossible to sneeze
with your eyes open*
—Anon.

My Father's Father

My cousin told me our grandfather had a heart attack when he was forty-five. He stopped hauling grain, produce and lumber with his horses and wagon; put most of his nine children to work; sat by the coal fire, listening to the Brunswick radio and frequently taking his pulse; and lived to the ripe old age of ninety-four.

Only two of his children lived to that age. □

My father's family before leaving Ontario to come West (pre-WWI). My father is first on the left (front row) and his father, Robert George, is third from the left (back row)

Thin Ice Skaters

Let me tell you, dear reader, there are some women who are thin-ice skaters. No matter the danger, they swirl through life ignoring the cracks and chips. They go where they want, and in the way they want, or at least that's the impression they leave. I knew one such woman who, when I'd been around her awhile, reminded me of Elizabeth Taylor—she, not unlike Elizabeth, loved babies, animals and men, and they all loved her. She had a sensuous vigour I'd not seen in my small world. She was bright and so funny. It had never occurred to me that these qualities would attract men, but they did, like fly-paper.

She and her engineer husband had emigrated from Australia, and our small city, very quickly, embraced them as civic treasures: he, with his quiet, wise comments and obvious professional competency; she, with her auburn-haired glow that lit any room she was in.

Ordinarily, a woman who looked as she did would be self-centred but not "E." She was asked to celebrity model, do puppeting at hospitals, M.C. at fund-raisers and sing in a madrigal group. She kept rabbits, boarded a very live python when its owner left town, had babies and nursed them at mixed meetings—even before Margaret Trudeau shocked the establishment with her "primitive behaviour"—cooked, cleaned and energized whomever she met. "G.," her husband, seemed to enjoy her aura.

One of my friends told me that "E." had said, "I can have any man I want, even *your* husband." In my naiveté, this side of her had never occurred to me; now I'm told she had more than one affair with smitten men in our city. □

Everybody is ignorant, only on different subjects

—Will Rogers (1879–1935).

TWEEZERED WORDS

words gripped with tweezers
silver, slant tipped and cold
visible word tips
grasped, yanked
like slivers from a thumb
plucked eyebrows.

with tweezers
she lays them on the page
a philatelist drawing
coloured squares from glassine envelopes.

holds her breath
places last paste rose
on top layer of wedding cake.

a steel-nerved diamond cutter
cut accomplished
lays glittering particles
in concentric circles on black velvet mats.

her final words tweezed onto pages
silver tool at rest.

Welsh Magic

I didn't know that Welsh blood in one's veins gives an extra amount of sensibility to an individual, but how else can the two events I am about to relate be explained?

My husband Hu, whose father was born in Wales, always said "I'm going to die with my boots on." We used to tease him about this statement, and we wondered how he was going to manage it, but he did. He died in the saddle, with his boots on, while completing a ride in a cutting horse contest.

When Hu's sister, a year older than him and mentally handicapped, was told of her brother's death, she had an unusual reaction. She told the staff at Deerhome Lodge, where she was living, "That's too bad, but I'll die on his birthday and go up to heaven to see him and mummy and daddy, too."

Less than three months later, on the eve of her brother's birthday, Muriel said good-bye to the hospital staff. The next morning, when she woke and found out she wasn't in heaven, she became very agitated. She fussed and fumed all day, had a heart attack and died. □

Whatever doesn't kill me,
makes me stronger

—Nietzsche (1844–1900).

FEATHER BOAS

A feather boa wound round her neck
Sarah McLachlan wails
I will remember you.

The faint pulse at
her throat
throbbing to
Will you remember me?

While the feather boa
trembles
like a rose petal ruffling
softly urging her on
its days at the end
of a flaunting ostrich tail over.

Sarah's boa black.
Auntie Mame's red
flung over a shoulder
slinking down a long staircase on her way to yet
another man.

And the way a boa
is only worn by women.
No trim for men's dinner jackets or
turtlenecks.

Feminine meringue cloud soft
soothing, sexy, scintillating.
Call of the siren
when she flicks the length
and pulls it through her hands.
Simmering female wiles rise
higher on a thermometer
to red-hot boiling hard ball cracking stage.

The feather boa
does its job.

Poetry is the stuff in books
that doesn't
quite reach the margins

—Anonymous child's essay.

vineyard
dreams

Two adults sit on a flaking white porch, which is perched next to the bay. One is a slim woman of about fifty in white shorts and a blue T-shirt with "Hu's Woo 30" on the front in red; the other is a handsome man of about fifty-six, his T-shirt reading "Joyce's Choice 30." Both are sitting on deck chairs, each in a curved tailbone position, with their legs sticking straight out. The weather had been scorching hot earlier that day, but now there was a softness, moist and still, in the warm night air.

Have you seen such an August sky? Clear, with so many stars—like a child would dot with a straight up-and-down pencil in a clenched fist on a large sheet of newsprint.

Have you ever seen such a moving sky? It seems as if every few minutes a shooting star arcs down. Have you ever wondered why you didn't keep track of those wishes or—even if you could remember half of them—why some wishes would be golden and true while others turn blue and wrong?

Can you see the chicken wire nailed between the old wooden porch railing, somewhat spoiling the daytime view of Penticton at the end of the lake, but keeping a one-and-a-half-year-old grandson from falling to the beach below?

Can you hear the couple talking softly, softly so as not to disturb the stillness, except for the occasional dropping pine cone, rustling night animal, lapping waves or swooping bat?

The man speaks of moving land, dropping its powdery beige Okanagan silt in the gullies, making new areas on which to plant vineyards. "Vineyards are for grandchildren," he says.

How could she have known then what would happen—that she would end up alone, a gentlewoman of reduced circumstances, with no ownership in these vineyards, and children and their spouses mediating about the operation and ownership of the property? □

Northern Lights

Our family didn't have a typical Sunday routine, except for the biting cold, blue-skied days when we did our Sunday turn at Hidden Bar Ranch.

The cattle's breath fogged the corrals, and their manure plopped steaming onto the lumpy, frozen ground. My snowmobile-suited husband tried to get his team of one shivering wife and five eager children to help move the beasts for separating before shipping or doctoring.

I wondered why we were doing this work—other than for a tenuously anticipated profit, and for the fact that Hu "had to," that it was in his bones and that we were teaching the children that "work can be satisfying, God's in his Heaven, and all's right with the world."

I guess it is, but personally I prefer my work to be in other places, such as the kitchen. But I have to admit that I do think God can see and hear us better under the poplar trees, with urgent commands being shouted from humans and the crackling, bellowing music of working cattle on a crisp, cold afternoon.

Later, after a big dinner, we'd sleepily pack up and go load the car for the trip home to town. The nights were black, except for those silent, rolling, flowing, dancing, pink, green and white, magical Northern Lights above us. We would stand and watch, knowing how insignificant we were, but also knowing how thankful we were to be us and to have had such a day. □

My First Crush

It was so long ago. He had heavy-lidded, brown eyes and shiny, dark hair falling over his forehead. A young man who could toss his head.

My first crush at fourteen.

I dreamed of his solid chest, so much bigger than mine, in its green shirt, and the way he strolled to school with me following at a distance. I considered him an "older man."

He disappeared.

What happened to him?

I have an uneasy feeling that he may be somewhere living as a woman with a famous poet, and they both wear capes, one black, one red, and his voice is rich and low.

Now, of course, I don't understand why I thought him romantic. □

*It's possible to lead
a cow upstairs,
but not downstairs*

—Anon.

The Missing Belt Buckle

When Lori was four, she rode in her first horse show at the old Edmonton Gardens in a class called, "Walk-trot Western, under eight."

I'll never forget her on that day—perched on Penny, our old ranch horse who had a sweet disposition, Lori's hands gripping the horn of the scuffed western saddle. She had industriously scrubbed and rubbed it with saddle soap the day before the show, using every little bit of elbow grease she possessed. The reins dangled unevenly, and her short legs gripped Penny's ample sides. Her cowboy boots were not much longer than the width of the clumsy stirrups. A turquoise cowboy hat hid most of her blond curls and shaded her determined little face. She wore half-tucked-in, rumpled, turquoise jeans and a pink and white–flowered cowboy shirt, all making her look like a seasoned contestant of the times.

We saw her leaning forward slightly to pat Penny's withers and could tell she was talking to her. Afterwards, she told us she was saying, "Good girl, Penny. Good for you. Good for you."

Intently, she listened to the ringmaster's shouted commands: "Walk on…trot…wa-alk…reverse…halt…line up in the centre of the ring."

Then, when the little contestants were told to come forward, each grinning child received a ribbon. Lori got a white one for third place, and she got a bronze belt buckle (which she still has).

In the car on the way home, she clutched her satin ribbon with "Edmonton Horse Show, 3rd place" embossed in gold down the ribbon length. It was half the length of her arm, and the belt *buckle made in Germany weighed more than her tiny cowboy belt. When we were barely stopped in our driveway, she bolted out of the car and proudly showed our next-door neighbour, Mr. Johnston, her spoils. He stopped raking his lawn, admired the buckle, patted her head and said, "Good for you, dear."*

Next she trotted off to show the Rooneys, the neighbours on our other side, but somehow, in four-year-old fashion, she lost her first trophy buckle. Her big green eyes overflowed with tears, and Mr. Johnston, hearing her sobs, called out, "Lori, I'm offering a reward to anyone who finds it." He probably thought a sibling had borrowed it.

Fifteen minutes later, a beaming Lori rushed back to the Johnstons to claim the reward—she'd found the buckle herself, though I don't remember where. A smiling Mr. Johnston rose to the occasion and handed her a quarter.

It wasn't as though she was getting something for nothing. □

It is the highest creatures who take the longest to mature, and are the most helpless during their immaturity

—George Bernard Shaw (1856–1950).

when
I was little

When I was a little girl growing up in what was the small city of Edmonton, it wasn't so long ago—I didn't travel in a covered wagon, and I didn't ride a horse to school, and my school's bathroom was down the hall, just like yours is, not in a little building behind the school—but some things were different from what you know now.

Milk only came in glass bottles, and it was delivered to our back door early every morning except Sunday. Our milk-man drove a wagon pulled by a team of two horses, and since

for my grandchildren: Bill, Stephanie, Tommy, Lori, Tasli, Lucas,
Kyli, Molly, Annie, Hu, Rosie, Katie, Angus and Maggie

I was asleep or dozing when they came, all I saw of the horses was the manure they often left in our dirt lane. Sometimes, though, I'd hear them snort and I'd also hear the clinking noise of the bottles in the metal carrying basket. The empties rattled more than full bottles did. Milk was paid for with cardboard tickets or metal tokens.

The cream in milk wasn't mixed in, like it is today (that's called homogenization). It floated to the top of the bottle, and in the middle of winter, when it was very cold, the frozen cream would pop through the bottle opening, rising like the pale half of a banana, and it would still have the little, round cardboard lid with its brown pull tab sitting on top like a flat hat. When my mother brought the bottle in, she would slice off this cream chunk and put it in a small, crackled pitcher to thaw for our breakfast porridge.

After I finished my porridge, I had to take a big spoonful of Scots Emulsion, which was a fishy, oily concoction that all the children on my block took in the winter. You're lucky; you can take Flintstone vitamins that taste and look like candy, and drink orange juice.

We didn't have a fridge until I was quite old, and then it had its motor on top in a big, round bump. The fridge had four tiny ice cube trays we thought were wonderful because to make ice before—when we had an ice box in the basement—required a big chunk of ice in the top half of the ice

177

box. My mother or dad would use a sharp ice pick to chip pieces for lemonade. The big chunk of ice would gradually melt into a tube that drained into a pan under the shelves and had to be carefully emptied I don't know how often. My mother put a sign reading "ice" in the window of the porch to signal whether we needed this summer commodity. The ice was delivered by Bill, the ice-man, who wore a blue shirt, had a black mustache and was very strong. He wore a black rubber cape because after he'd lifted a big block of ice from the back of the wagon with huge tongs, he would twirl it over his shoulder where it rested on his rubber-covered back. Then he'd clunk down our basement steps and thunk it into place in the ice box. We paid in tickets purchased when we could afford them. The ice came from the river in winter, when men with horse-drawn sleighs would saw blocks of clear river ice, pile them high in the sleighs and take them to an ice house. Here, they would stay frozen between wood shavings until another river freeze-up, when more could be harvested.

There was no such thing as an automatic dishwasher when I was a child, just a white enamel dishpan, soap flakes or a bar of soap, a dishcloth, steel wool, Dutch cleanser, baking soda, tea towels and, when I was older, we got a dish rack to balance the clean dishes on. We also had a small triangular strainer to put peelings and unused food in. This wet garbage was wrapped into parcels of newspaper and put in brown paper bags and then into a barrel in the back lane. Once a week a horse-drawn garbage wagon would come and the men would toss it through the air, like they do today. It was very smelly because the garbage wasn't in green bags as it is nowadays.

We didn't have anything plastic, except some small toys. The only one I can remember is a pink kewpie doll made of celluloid. There wasn't as much garbage when I was a child because things didn't come packaged like they do today. A toothbrush didn't have a box around it. Rice for rice pudding didn't come in a plastic bag. We didn't have juice boxes. Socks weren't stuck together with sticky labels and in sealed bags. There weren't big crackling boxes for toys.

Our washing machine was different. When I was very little, my mother washed our clothes by rubbing and scrubbing them over a scrub board, a corrugated metal sheet set in a wooden frame. She had big wash tubs, which she drained into the basement drain. Later, she got a washing machine which had white rubber rollers. When she pushed the wet clothing between them, the water was squeezed out. To dry the clothes, she'd take them in a creaking wicker basket to the backyard, where she had a little platform. She'd climb up three steps to a pole with a wired crosspiece that she pinned the clothes to with special metal-hinged wooden pegs. Our clothesline was something like a big strong spiderweb on a pole. In the winter, the wet clothes would be frozen and she would bring them in, stiff as boards but smelling of such fresh cold that I wish I could have perfume just like it. Then she would re-hang them in the basement to finish drying.

If I was sick with measles, mumps or whooping cough, a man from the health department would come and put a sign on our front door warning people that I had a disease and no children could come to play with me. When I was sick, I stayed in bed; we didn't have medicine like you have now to make you better faster. Sometimes if I had a bad cold or strep throat, my aunt came and made a paste of mustard and flour and put it on my chest and then covered it with flannel and it got so hot and stung. And sometimes my mother would wrap a wet, white, long stocking around my neck and cover it with another cloth and give me lemon juice and honey and rub me all over with alcohol to cool down a fever. Sometimes, she'd give me enemas; I cried and cried when she did that.

There was no such thing as T.V. when I was little, but we did have a radio, and attached to it, on top, was a record player. There were no personal computers when I was a child, although there were typewriters. They were always black. There was no such thing as a microwave oven or a gas barbecue. We cooked and heated food on the stove and had toasted marshmallows over a campfire. Our house didn't have a wood-burning fireplace; it had a gas radiant that was lit in the winter and glowed orange and blue and was very hot; I was never, never to touch its starter handle.

The only time I had a spanking was when I played outside too late, until after the street lights were on. I came home and my parents were out looking for me so I hid under the spare room bed. My daddy found me and spanked me and said, "Don't you *ever* frighten your mummy and daddy like that again." I've remembered it for more than sixty years. In the olden days parents and some teachers spanked children, but it didn't mean they didn't still love them.

Most people didn't have cars. Our family shared one with my cousin Jack's family. Often, people used the buses like they do today, but more often, they used the streetcars, which ran on rails like train tracks and were attached by a long pole to overhead wires. Sometimes blue sparks came from the top of this pole when it came to a crossing. People didn't go on holidays in an airplane. Planes were just two-seaters without roofs and didn't fly as high as they do today. There weren't any jets.

When I was little, I didn't have a lot of clothes like you kids have today. And girls didn't wear pants to school. When I was older, I had ski pants, but I still had a skirt or dress

underneath. I didn't have running shoes when I was quite young, and children never wore black or purple like you do. My aunts sometimes sent me clothes that my older cousins had outgrown and once, they sent me a beautiful patchwork jacket made of all different colours of velvet patches. I'd like one just like it now. It had lots of red and flowered velvet in it. I wonder what happened to it after I got too big to wear it? I hope another little girl wore it and loved it as much as I did.

For fun, I played games with my friends. I remember sitting in the shade on the grass between two friends' houses, playing cards. We used wooden matches for chips, and we were bitten all over by mosquitoes but I never did get red bumps like my friend Daurel. She had little dots of baking soda paste on her itchy spots. Through the years of my childhood I had a teddy bear called "Teddy," whose tummy when squeezed played "Oh where, oh where has my little dog gone?" a stuffed pink and white dog called "Sweetheart," a small rubber baby doll called Joanna and another doll, Shirley Temple. I had a red tricycle and later a red two-wheeler bike, a toboggan, a yo-yo, a bolo bat and a lacrosse ball for throwing up against the side of the house to play "plain, fancy; one hand, the other hand; one foot, the other foot; tweedle, twydle; front-back, back-front; curtsy, salute; roundabout." I had a skipping rope, a baseball and bat, skates (roller—which were all metal and had a key I wore around my neck on a string along with my bicycle lock key), ice skates, skis that fastened on my boots with thick rubber bands and a small, blue bookshelf my cousin Gordon made me with a few books in it. That bookshelf is in Lori and Annie's bedroom now. And we went to the southside library, too. So I was a very lucky child.

When my friends couldn't play with me and since I didn't have brothers or sisters to play with, my parents would read to me and play games with me. I went mushroom hunting with my daddy, and he took me to the racetrack. My mummy let me help her sometimes when she was making cookies, and I would eat some of the dough raw. She taught me how to knit, embroider and to paint with water colours, but I really didn't like doing any of those things very much. I think I wasn't very patient, and she was so very good at doing them, she made it look so easy. When I tried, I was all thumbs and my hands would get so hot and sticky and I would drop stitches, my embroidery needle would come un-threaded and my water colours always ran together and looked like mud because I wouldn't wait long enough.

Mrs. Mills (we always called adults Mr. or Mrs., not their first names) was the mother of my two friends, Elsie Muriel and Daurel, and she told us how to put on a play. It was a famous story called "A Midsummers Night's Dream" and I was a fairy. Along with other friends Audrey, Beth and Josephine, we did this one summer in the park and also in a thick woods where a big university building for teachers now stands. We spent hours and hours learning our lines, and when it was our turn to come on stage, and where we should stand, and how we should move. And we had *such* a good time.

I've seen some of you perform in school and dance recitals and after you've gone to day-camps and have learned some neat songs. It always reminded me of fun I had when I was little.

Once my parents and my aunt and uncle rented a cabin at Pigeon Lake. Our cabin didn't have running water, but there was a water pump at the end of the street where we could move a heavy handle up and down until icy cold water would gush out and fill the pails. It was such hard work, my cousin Jackie and I both had to hold onto the handle and sort of jump up and then pull down. We really needed a drink by the time we finished. Down a path in the backyard there was an outdoor toilet that didn't flush. I was always afraid I would fall in, and it was so smelly. If we had to go in the night, there were special white bowl things with handles that our mothers would empty in the morning. We didn't have a bath or shower so we got clean in the lake. What we loved was when it was stormy and the foamy waves would knock us down and then when we were all cold and shivery we'd go back to the cabin to dry off, and dress in front of a big fire. Then we'd have hot cocoa and play either Snakes & Ladders or Chinese checkers. There weren't any lights—just coal oil lamps so we had to be very very careful, because if they were tipped, they could set the house on fire.

You see, things were different when I was little, but a lot of things were the same. I had parents who loved me and looked after me, grandparents, aunts, uncles and cousins to visit, and friends to play with. Nothing wrong with that. □

We are all born charming,
fresh and spontaneous.
We just need civilizing

—Anon.

AS THOUGH TO A CHILD

As though to a child
I want to say
Turn those mouth corners up
up
up.
Wrinkle patterns
make me guess
not many smiles
crack that lonely face
though I've seen her
with a man at Safeway
and he seemed to be lecturing her
as though to a child.

Her mouth drooped
even further
down
down
down
tough tough.

A creased, not folded neck
held her unbent head
glinting behind thick glasses
magnified memories
mesh in her mind
dates tumble
make no sense
what difference does it make
who did what when
they did it and it was good?

and she smiled.

The Dinner

Short-stemmed, white tulips in a black glass bowl decorated the mahogany table. Honey-scented beeswax candles were burning low. Three couples sat around the table in various relaxed positions: the husbands, Malcolm, David and Stephan, were all in the English department at the city's university; the wives had various jobs—Zoe, a nurse on extended leave from hospital downsizing, Linda, a feature writer for a local paper, and Rebecca, a singer-actress who was unemployed. The six of them had just finished a four-hour dinner hosted by Stephan and Rebecca. This dinner occurred monthly, with rotating hosts. Rebecca, who did everything with flare, had set before them a deceptively simple meal of stuffed chicken and steamed vegetables. Only scattered crumbs remained from the black olive and walnut bread she had made that morning.

Malcolm held the floor. All three men were extremely articulate and inclined to interrupt their wives, even other men's wives. David and Stephan, however, could rarely get the better of Malcolm. He, of the loudest voice, often talked right over, around and above any brave soul's interjections. As is the case with many opinionated people, he was insensitive to the shift of changing moods. So it was most strange that Malcolm and Zoe had, all of their married lives, been very careful not to say, but only indicate, to each other, what

Pure logic is the ruin of the spirit

—Antoine de Saint-Exupéry (1900–44).

they were thinking. Zoe had to guess frequently what was on his mind and wondered if he had ever tried to read hers.

The women had lifted the remains of the dinner to the sideboard. A large chicken carcass sat in a yellow casserole dish with dark brown onion and garlic stuck to its walls. A small amount of butter congealed on a white asparagus platter. The empty chocolate soufflé dish had a sticky brown rim, where the fragrant concoction had stuck. The last of three bottles of a '94 Mission Hills chardonnay sat empty on the table. A cheese board, with a small slice of asiago and some bare grape stems, sat next to a split of ice wine, almost empty, its fragrant contents sipped slowly and appreciatively from tiny tumblers.

Malcolm's voice, with its great carrying qualities, boomed over the company: "Did you hear about Jean in Linguistics? She's resigned from the Department. God, can you *believe* Stan had no idea? *No one* could be *that* blind, deaf and dumb."

Zoe licked her index finger, pressed it on scattered crumbs around her place, licked it, and slowly repeated this movement. Then she detected an unknown wild tone when Malcolm repeated, "*No one* could be *that* blind, deaf and dumb." Their eyes met. The smug feeling she'd lived with these past weeks dissolved, and she knew he knew, and it would be over. □

A Farmers' Market

I'm reminded of backstage, just before a performance. That tension and anticipation. A collective look at the clock and a rolling of the eyes skyward, as "Showtime" nears.

We're at the Strathcona Farmers' Market just before 8 A.M., about to sell our wares to the customers who plod through snowdrifts in parking lots, under street lights glowing in the early morning darkness. It's bitterly cold, two Saturdays before Christmas, and for vendors like me, the best two days for sales in the whole year.

I've finished setting out my "Through the Grapevine" dried flower and silk flower baskets and French beribboned grapevine wreaths as well as my homemade foods: vinegars—nasturtium, lemon thyme and basil—apricot chutney, pickled cherries, sweet and sour pepper jelly, lemon curd and Christmas tapanade. I'm semi-satisfied with my display, though I wish I could bring myself to "production-line" my flower and fruit creations—then I'd be able to put just one or two prototypes on splendid display. I hope having too much selection isn't confusing. Yards of heavy, dark green fabric, covered partially with white, embroidered and lace cloths, seemed appropriate when I first envisioned the display. I put empty florist boxes underneath it all to give different levels for the baskets, bottles and jars. For an amateur in this world, I've learned a bit, but I know I've got a long way to go.

The stall next to mine is obviously occupied by a begin-
ner, a nervous, red-headed woman with a pale, freckled little
boy who also has red hair. Both of them are neatly dressed
and tight with excitement. Their table is crowded with a single layer of the mother's wares: pink and blue knitted baby
sweaters, bonnets and booties, tiny baskets of dried baby's
breath with red ribbons, jars of Saskatoon jelly and dill pickles, embroidered tea towels made from bleached flour sacks,
good-looking gingersnaps and chocolate fudge in plastic bags
with red ribbons.

My heart cramps when I think of the effort she's gone to,
the gamble she's taking, buying stall space at this time of the
year. I wonder if this effort is how she's going to give her son
a good Christmas if her gamble pays off. Just before the doors
open for business, she clears a small space on the table for her
little boy to play with his tiny trucks, crayons and colouring
book. She gives him a bottle of orange pop and a cookie and
gently explains, "I'll be very busy, and I know you'll be a good
boy." He settles in to play, but he soon knocks over the pop,
where it spreads its bright orangeness across the white cloth
and touches the tiny, knitted garments. His mother screams,
"Bobby, Bobby, how *could* you be so clumsy?"

"I'm sorry, Mummy, I'm sorry, I'm sorry, I'm sorry."

Now she's red-haired flaming mad. Who knows how important the results of this day could be for them. Maybe her husband, if she has one, has told her she's foolish to try this venture. She pushes her son out of the way and does her best to blot and mop, tearfully removing a few stained clothes from the table top to the floor behind her.

The public start to throng down our aisle, and I make some good sales, some to people who've bought from me before. I watch when I can, the red-head and her little boy. She's not used to selling. I think the not-unkind glances of passing people must seem to her to be from sneering city folk. Her shoulders are sinking, and she can't summon a smile. Her little boy sits idly, red eyed and quiet. She finally makes a small sale of a pair of pink booties and some fudge and I think, "Mm, maybe it'll turn out all right."

The market manager patrols the aisles making sure no rules are broken and that all is well. She stops next to me and talks earnestly to the young mother, whose face reddens, and I can sense her hair is bristling. After the manager leaves, she turns to the little boy and hisses, "Do you know what you've done? I might go to jail just because you were so clumsy."

Tears flow from mother and son, and I ask, "What's wrong?"

"Someone reported on me and said I was cruel to him, and they might have to tell the authorities."

I felt my own hair bristling. "Don't you worry, I saw and heard the whole thing. Here's my card. If there's trouble, I'll tell them you're a thoughtful mother and *no* one could have kept cool when an accident like yours happened."

After three o'clock, when we're all packed up, I can tell the quiet pair have had their fill of the Farmers' Market. I hope they've made something more than their expenses, and she won't need to phone me to vouch for her.

I've watched for them at the market ever since, and I've wondered if the slap this young woman received was just one of many in her short life. I'm sure it was. I'm sure she is a good mother. Just not a perfect one. □

Only 30 percent of us can flare our nostrils.

fluttering
words

My parents' words bounce in my brain like fluttering badminton birds—clicking, ticking, flicking, falling—but calling to me:

"No means no."

"Don't touch."

"Why? Because I said so."

"Do unto others as you would have others do unto you."

"Calm down."

"Hold your temper."

"Don't say anything if you can't say anything nice."

"No, you can't have a baby brother or sister."

"Push your soup spoon away from you."

"Break your bun in pieces and butter each piece in turn."

"Chew with your mouth closed."

"Don't be a fibber."

"Did you remember your manners?"

"A four-leaf clover for good luck—make a wish."

"That's not very nice."

"Don't you dare stick out your tongue at me."

"Don't make a funny face when you talk—it might stick that way."

"No, this mushroom has bugs."

"Ladybug, ladybug, fly away home."

"Look a person in the eyes when you talk to her."

"You'll catch more flies with honey than with vinegar."

"You first wind the wool around your little finger, like this."

"Don't call older people by their first names, like we do."

"Stand up when older people enter the room."

"Fifteen-two, fifteen-four, and two is six and one for his nibs."

"Don't slouch."

"This is called cobalt blue."

"Straighten up."

"I'll rub your back till you fall asleep."

"Don't forget your scarf."

"Wear your over-boots. There are still puddles."

"They're called forget-me-nots, and they're as blue as the sky, aren't they?"

"No. Finish your practising."

"Do we have to listen to Frank Sinatra all the time?"

"Have you done your homework?"

"Take off that gold safety pin on your slip strap. What if you were in an accident?"

"Just kid them along."

"Nice girls don't swear."

"Nice girls don't sit like that."

"Be in before midnight for sure."

"Are you smoking?"

"Did you have something to drink?"

"Who introduced you?"

And so at nineteen, I married and left home.

My parents were smiling. My mother had no need to shed a single tear. She was not one to do so in public anyway; her way was more buttoned up. And the only time I'd seen my dad with tears was when he was hit in the eye by a softball. (Occasionally, he could be persuaded to fill in at a scrub baseball game, the only father to do so.) My friend Audrey felt terrible, but it was just an accident, and dad said the sun was in his eyes and that was what made them water.

I've heard it said that a person's character is basically formed by the age of six. I think the thirty-eight years I spent at my husband's side were every bit as influential in warping and woofing my fabric as were the nineteen years with my gentle parents.

It's funny though; badminton bird words from Hu do not hover in my head in the same clear way that those older words have. □

Just remember you're unique,
just like everyone else

—Anon.

four-leaf
clovers

Today I went to the cemetery. I don't go that often, but it's August the seventh, and Hu and I would be celebrating our fiftieth wedding anniversary.

It's been hot, almost like days in the Okanagan. I have to water the tomatoes and petunias twice a day on my little patios. I'm going to try for the ugliest specimen next month at the Royal Tomato Society contest. There's no way any of my tomatoes are going to be eligible for the heaviest category.

On the way to the cemetery, I scrambled down the riverbank at Emily Murphy Park to get a rock for a friend's rock garden. She and her husband were married the same day we were, and a rock garden was how they wanted to mark the celebration. The park was quiet. I only saw one runner, a sinewy young mother pushing a sleeping child in a fancy yuppie stroller. I got the rock, to be washed and taken to the party tonight, and went on to the graveyard.

My parents, my husband and our first son are side by side, under the shade of two old spruce trees and now green, velvet grass. Their gravestones are the flat "stepping stone" style. While the grass surrounding them was well cut, at Hu's stone, an errant clump of clover had crept past the border on its way to hide the word "memory" in "To memory ever dear." I pulled at it and its straggling off-shoots.

My father's stone also had a clover clump over an edge. I smiled when I remembered that my dad had a habit of four-leaf clover sleuthing. He was sharp-eyed, and never did wear glasses. He was not above licking an extra clover leaf and placing it on a "four." Then he would tell me and my friends he'd found a five-leaf clover, and he'd say "Think how lucky it must be!"

As I weeded, I watched, and there it was, a tiny good-luck four-leaf clover. Carefully, I put it between pages in my chequebook, an impermanent and crass location, though all I could think of at the time. There was no creeping clover at my mother's or little Tommy's gravestone.

I thought, *What if I've thrown away good luck from Hu's clover clump?* I went back, sifting through the now limp stalks and bits, and found one medium-sized clover leaf, wrinkled but definitely four petalled. Another lucky four-leaf clover to press—reminding me of two of the five most important men in my life.

Hu always said, "You make your own good luck." I can hardly wait to see what's going to happen. □

I CARE

I care.

Of course, I care.

Don't I

wake in the night?

your name

tripping

in my brain.

I wake in the night

hold book on high

the words

my memory-blocker.

At dawning

the unthinkable.

No Rhubarb about Rhubarb

"Rhubarb" may be another name for an argument, but you'll get no argument from me about the goodness of early spring rhubarb.

Years ago, when rhubarb's pink knobs pushed through a garden's warming earth, mothers watched until the stalks were at least a foot tall, pulled the rhubarb wands from their slots with a clicking sound, whacked off the poisonous umbrella leaves, and carried the pink treasures to their kitchens. There, they chopped, cooked and sugared them. The mothers said, "It's *so* good for you, dears. It's your spring tonic."

Brits refer to rhubarb as "nanny food," but that's because when they were very young they were obliged to eat a tangled mass of it on top of a congealed blob of Harry Horn's custard powder. As adults, these folk should try soft custard or yogurt with a baked rhubarb compote on the side—rhubarb, oven-stewed in its own juices, with no added water (though a few squirts of orange juice and some honey are good additions). Or they could sprinkle the rhubarb with toasted flaked almonds on top of the honey.

Do you remember sitting on your back step with your best friend, each of you dipping a stalk of rhubarb in a cracked teacup of sugar? Can you still feel that intense, sweet-sour puckering in your mouth, as though your cheeks might be sucked inside-out at any minute? Remember how your knees—not yet tanned from the spring sun, though freshly scabbed from falling from your bike—were pulled up near your chin and your lips were sugar coated, and you didn't have a care in the world?

The Recipes

Rhubarb Muffins

Set oven to 350° F.

Combine in a large bowl:
2 1/2 c. flour
1 tsp. baking soda
1/2 tsp. salt

Combine in a bowl and add to above:
1 1/4 c. brown sugar
1/2 c. canola or grapeseed oil

Mix (but don't overmix) and add to above:
1 egg
1 c. buttermilk
1 tsp. vanilla

Fold into above:
1 tbsp. grated orange rind
2 c. small, diced rhubarb

Fill 20 greased or lined muffin tins about 3/4 full with batter. Sprinkle sugar on top of each and bake at 350° F for 20–25 minutes or until firm to the touch.

Rhubarb Crisp

Set oven to 350° F.

Toss in a 3-qt. baking dish:
8 c. diced rhubarb
1 1/4 c. sugar
1 tbsp. orange zest

Combine and stir into above:
2 tbsp. cornstarch
1/4 c. Cointreau

Set aside baking dish.

Mix in a bowl with hands or pastry blender until crumbly:
2 c. flour
3/4 c. cold butter, cut into small pieces
1 c. rolled oats
3/4 c. brown sugar
2 tsp. cinnamon
pinch salt

Fold into above:
3/4 c. slivered almonds
1 beaten egg

Spread flour mixture over rhubarb in baking dish. Bake for 50 minutes at 350° F or until the rhubarb bubbles and is tender and the top is golden. Serve warm with vanilla ice cream. Serves 6. □

WHEN I THINK OF IT ALL

When I think of it all
I smile.
I can see and feel king-sized hotel beds
not like our old-fashioned double at home.
How many?
More than a hundred?
Yes, way more.
No children to disturb us
heaven.
"Do not disturb" signs on doorknobs
till phone call to room service
and I hide under the covers
knowing what the young waiter thinks he knows but
   can't know
what's been happening in the rumpled bed
with the bedspread and my nightie on the floor.

No wonder I smile
I was married
to a romantic.

He stroked me with his
hands
tongue
and thoughts.

He talked
poems to me.

I cry sweet tears
Few of his poems are on paper.

One Thing Leads to Another

Last week I made lemon curd—quite a bit of it. It took six eggs, plus two egg yolks, half a pound of butter, twelve tablespoons of fresh lemon juice and two tablespoons of lemon zest. That left me with two egg whites, so I decided to make cocoa meringue kisses, which needed six egg whites, which left me with four egg yolks, so I made cookies with four egg yolks and one whole egg and in this baking managed to use up the last of a bag of dried cranberries, the last of a bag of dried apricots (cut in slivers with scissors), the last of a bag of walnuts and the last of a jar of toasted coconut.

That's pretty much the end of the story, but I got thinking about how life is just one thing leading to another. If we can remember what's in the bags and how one recipe for action affects another, maybe we'll fumble our way through, tasting the most delicious and having a lot to share and in the end be even.

Professionals built the Titanic,
amateurs the ark

—Anon.

The Recipes

For the lemon curd recipe, see page 110.

Cocoa Meringue Kisses

Set oven to 225° F.

Whip until stiff:
6 egg whites
1/4 tsp. salt

Gradually mix into above:
1 c. sugar.

Mix together:
2 tsp. water
2 tsp. vanilla

Whipping egg-white mixture constantly, alternately add
vanilla (a few drops at a time) and 1 more cup of sugar.

Fold in:
6 tbsp. cocoa

Drop batter on parchment-covered baking sheets. Bake
at 225° F until the kisses are partly dry and retain their
shape. Remove from pan while hot.

End Result Cookies

Set oven to 350° F.

Cream together:
2/3 c. butter
1/2 c. brown sugar
1/2 c. white sugar
1/2 tsp. vanilla
4 egg yolks
1 whole egg

Mix together and then add to above:
1/2 c. flour
1/2 tsp. baking soda
1 tsp. baking powder
1/4 tsp. salt
1/2 tsp. cinnamon
1/4 tsp. cardamom

Mix together and then combine with above:
1 1/2 c. asst. chopped nuts, dates, raisins, dried cranberries, apricots, pears or whatever.

Place small spoonfuls of dough on parchment-covered cookie sheets. Bake at 350° F for about 15 minutes. Watch before 15 minutes and change pan positions if necessary.

Makes more than four dozen cookies. □

OLD SKIN

A tiny grandchild strokes the back of my hand
lifting skin with feather fingers.

I think of blue-veined chickens ready for the oven.

The warm raised wrinkle
inelastic as flattened welting on a slipcover
slowly subsides as though exhausted.

Not so long ago, skin coated my bones like drizzled
icing on a cake.

It happened overnight.
One day young
the next
old.

But the child laughs and says it's funny.

Does it do that on your *feet*?

PICKERS' COOKIES AND TEA
For Judi Hindsen's birthday

In my head I draw

the long, green rows of your orchards

the pea hens

the violets in spring grass

the tea tray on a tree stump

under the mulberry tree

the herb patch

where I clip basil, marjoram, lavender and thyme

and you hold two buckets

of iris clumps.

Six more boxes of your green thumb miracles ready

for my car.

You bring me flats of strawberries

your hands stained by their warm juice.

The long table in your kitchen offers

pickers' cookies and tea.

Your mothering my daughter Lori
after Kyli was born
and we don't know
of her MS diagnosis.
Your comforting hugs
for my daughter
while I live at the other end of the telephone.
Knowing the difficult life you juggle
with husband's creeping Alzheimer's.
Your South African stories and laughter.

Though our days together have been few
I receive your generosity of spirit
with love and thanks.
I hope I've drawn
but not sucked strength from you.

Sixty-nine-Year-Old Me
Talking to my Body

Me: O.K., old dear, you realize you've got a few problems, don't you?

Body: Well, I guess—they're my *knees* and the ankle is the way it is because you insisted on having that last glass of wine and then you said the bottom step was shorter than the one above.

Me: But honestly, that's the truth and it's *me* who goes to the physio and the arthritis doctor and had the bone scan and takes the pills at 5:30 in the morning so I'll have an empty stomach before and after, and let me say, if you had been in better condition, the ligaments would have snapped back into position right smartly, and we wouldn't be having this silly conversation.

Body: Then what about the latest cholesterol count? You've been pretty smug, telling me you're eating healthy. How did *this* happen, huh?

Me: Can't you see, madam-chicken-before-the-egg? I haven't been able to do the fast walking like I did before the test, when the count went down. All because of your inelastic tendons.

Body: We're starting to sound like a couple in conflict, and don't tell me I need a Prozac. I just need you to realize you can't go on in this buzzed-up state and expect me to perform like a new Mercedes. □

There are three things
I always forget.
Names, faces and—the third
I can't remember

—Anon.

SLOW ON THE UPTAKE

I have trouble repeating jokes
or saying I understand

goat stubborn stalled words.

Reason does not spur them
nor do funny wine-soaked nights
nor hidden clues
from balance sheets
nor impassioned cries
loosen their grip on
my pudding lubricated slow-whirling gears.

No greasy logic or
total recall sucks them forth.

"Duh," they whisper.

"Duh."

"Duh."

*If you try to fail and succeed,
which have you done?*

—Anon.

This Year, Next Year, Sometime, Never.

Both when I was a child, and when my children were young, we would make a wish after we finished eating canned plums or cherries. Then we would sing-song the refrain, "This year, next year, sometime, never," while we counted the sucked-clean pits at the bottom of our mauve-pink tinted bowls. Whichever word was said when the last pit was touched would indicate the time when the wish would come true.

Nothing ever, in these kinds of games, was said of the past. Because of course, there's absolutely no use wishing "What if." That's only wondering, and we'll never know. There's still time to say, "I'll do it sometime." Try not to dwell on anything you *know* you will never do—like have more babies, or firm skin, or climb Mt. Everest, or study voice, though starting to write is a proven possibility. We inherit tendencies to create our futures, and life treats us better if we respond well to what's thrown at us.

If you are over sixty-five, you will understand me when I say, "Next year came faster this year than last." □

It's all very well to be able to write books, but can you waggle your ears?

—J.M. Barrie (1860–1937).

Those of Us Who

Those of us who remember golden childhoods, not nightmares.

Those of us who think of some bad spots in life so long ago, but on reflection, balance these bad moments with other, better ones.

Those of us who floated through early years with hardly a serious thought, though with fair instincts, taught by example.

Those of us who had no driving ambition of a glorious destiny, nor a strong will to accomplish and contribute.

Those of us who had some small leadership qualities but not that urge to organize and control.

Those of us who through mostly good luck fell into active roller coaster lives and thrived.

Those of us who found menopause interesting and heeded our mothers' advice of "Only people who talk about it suffer."

Those of us who accept widowhood as just one more phase of growing up and who can truly contemplate the past with a smile.

Those of us who recognize that getting older gives a freedom from embarrassing easily.

Those of us who realize some aches and pains are part of the ageing process and need to be accommodated.

Those of us who make sure they spend time around children and young adults, finding their viewpoints are more easily understood than they would have been twenty years ago.

Those of us who are in the approaching "old age world" and decide this time is one of the best in life. □

The best things in life aren't things
—Anon.

My Fabulous Fantasy Meal

My fabulous fantasy meal will be a lengthy affair in mid-September, held in a large room above Lake Okanagan at Paradise Ranch Vineyards. The chef will be Simon Smotkowicz, director of the award-winning Canadian Culinary Team. The guests will be my late husband, Hu Harries, because he loved superb food and conversation, and the other guests would enjoy his company; Salmon Rushdie, because he's so bright and funny; and M. F. K. Fisher, because she'd talk as she wrote—sensible, funny and terrifically tuned into food.

I was going to invite Colette, because she wrote so sensuously of food, but then I'd need a translator, so instead I've chosen Emma Thompson, because she's so bright and funny, and Gerald (not Lawrence) Durrell, because he was such a gutsy man and would fit this table well. I know we'll laugh a lot, and that's good for digestion.

As the guests gather, Tommy Banks will be playing the piano—George Gershwin, Cole Porter, Duke Ellington and whatever else he feels appropriate. He'll stop for a drink with us and play again at dessert and coffee time.

First, with Veuve Clicquot Grand Dame Champagne in Baccarat flutes (most of the stemware is Baccarat), we'll toast the fact that we're all here. Two caviars—Beluga and Iranian golden—will be served in imperial jade bowls, each bowl in crushed ice in another larger jade bowl, and we'll all stand around, each of us with an ancient ivory spoon, and help ourselves. A big, rough vine basket will be lined with a linen napkin and filled with saffron brioche, and we'll have pieces of it between spoonfuls of caviar. Tiny shots of icy vodka with twists of lemon rind or Krug Grande Cuvée champagne will be available for whomever wants either.

At the table, everyone will have a clear view of the lake and a comfortable, straight-backed chair. The tablecloth will be white Porthault linen with a dark green border, matching the extra-large napkins. The length of the table will be piled with bunches of green and red wine grapes still on the vine, with leaves, sitting on moss and full-blown roses of many hues nestled amongst the fruit. Cream-coloured votives and tall cream tapers will be in moss-covered holders.

We'll have a salad of wild leaves (picked while we're caviar-tasting) with warm eastern Canadian scallops, in a walnut-oil vinaigrette, served on Baccarat crystal plates. Accompanying the salad will be French bread baked that morning and flown over from Paris. The wine will be '81 Pouilly Blanc Fume la Doucette.

The main course, served on Royal Doulton white plates with dark green borders accompanied by George Jensen flatware, will be free-range chickens stuffed with lemon thyme and garlic, served on warm orzo cooked in chicken broth and sprinkled with chives and pulled-apart chive blossoms; bright green, shelled fresh fava beans, cooked and then squirted from their skins; red peppers grilled over grapevine cuttings, skinned and sliced into strips; a small triangle of wild mushrooms with sorrel in filo pastry; and sweet and sour (not hot) pepper jelly. The wine choices for this chicken course are a '92 Mission Hill Chardonnay (the Avery Award winner) or Louis Roederer Cristal Champagne '73.

By this time, the moon will be high and bright, making a shimmering white trail on the lake below us, and the bats will be swooping past the windows wondering what all the fuss is about.

Dessert will be four small gelato plops on the side of a quarter-pear baked with Poire William. Gelato flavours will be all wild fruits—saskatoon, raspberry, strawberry and blueberry—and a few of these berries will top each gelato flavour.

Orange mint will be finely shredded on top of the pear. The dessert will be on chilled amber plates, and a '67 Château d'Yquem will be offered in tiny, antique clear glasses.

A cheese selection of Stilton, *chèvre* and English cheddar will be offered with more Parisian bread, all from a huge Chinese tea basket lined with grape leaves. The plates used will be hand-carved and polished redwood. Cockburn's Vintage Port 1927 will be served.

Chef Simon will join us for cognac and coffee—Blue Mountain from Jamaica—and there'll be Remy Martin Centaur Louis XIII Cognac and a Miessen bowl of candied ginger. The wines will be passed around (and around) the table, though the table will be served and cleared by efficient young locals trained by Chef Simon. The portions of all foods, except the caviar, will be small.

The whole meal will be eaten by candle- and moonlight. □

The young have aspirations that never come to pass, the old have reminiscences of what never happened
—Saki (1870–1916).

I Mustn't

You know I can't. I mustn't even think about whose husbands are the most attractive. Don't get me wrong—I don't have eyes for any of them. I only have eyes for men in general, just like my Aunt Doris, though really, when you examined her closely, she had eyes for men in particular. She always wore red and poured a drink for the T.V. repair man. When I went to visit, the two of them were laughing and having a great old time and even in the nursing home she always had a man. When I visited with cousins, she would giggle if they were male, but we females didn't even get a smile.

So what am I doing alone? Maybe I'm not like my Aunt Doris—maybe I'm like my Aunt Ruby. God, I hope not. She was the old maid.

"Too fussy," my mother said. "Way too fussy." Aunt Ruby was asked, but the men were never good enough, so she ended up dressed all in black in the Millinery Department at Johnson Walkers, until she had to retire because she was cranky with the customers. I used to watch her, and when she said, "Madam, it's lovely," even I could tell that it was a lie dribbling from her lips. Ruby's eyes would be cold and madam would leave hatless. No beflowered, beribboned creation on her head. And my aunt, a sneer on her face, would turn on her heel, look in a mirror, smooth her hair, see me, and smile. Then we would go to Picardy's on Jasper Avenue for lunch. □

Women's hearts beat faster than men's

—bumper sticker.

The Food Grinder

When I was very young, my mother let me turn the handle. Chunks of carrots crunched, and the onions made me cry. The roast beef squiggled out like the pink-grey worms robins look for. Sunday fare was turning into shepherd's pie.

A tiny kitchen with a white metal table. My daddy would say, "Thanks girls—it's delicious," and we knew we would do it again.

But what I didn't know then, was that I would use my mother's grinder for many years until my children, children of another era—a bigger jump to newness than even between my mother's world and mine—would see me turning a switch instead of a handle, and a noisy, cruel blade would more quickly do the job a quiet duo did many years ago. □

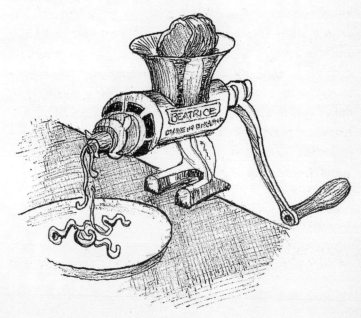

a recovered
widow

I am a recovered widow.

Not that I still don't have a crush on that
beautiful man I married fifty years ago
but I only smile inside now when I think of him.
Yet still
I wish he were at my side
and when I'm laughing with children and grandchildren
I wish he were at my side.
When I'm outside on a bright hoar-frosted morning
I wish he were still at my side.
When I see rows of grapevines laden with translucent
     bunches
and I think of the anguish
connected with this beautiful vineyard
I wish he were still at my side.
When I smell steak and kidney pie
I wish he were still at my side.
When I fly and find myself at baggage arrival with
     strangers
I wish he were still at my side.
And when I go to bed
after an evening out, I wish I were still at his side.

Otherwise, I'm a recovered widow.

about the author

Joyce Harries was born in 1928, a time when milkmen still delivered by horse and wagon and the iceman came around in the winter to deliver blocks of ice cut from the river. Joyce married at nineteen to Hu Harries, who taught economics at the university. To Joyce, their marriage was a true love story, not only resulting in six children but in a partnership that supported them both through thirty-eight years of marriage. Joyce and her family undertook many ventures, including owning 14,000 acres of ranchland in southern Alberta; Hu's political career, both as an Edmonton city alderman and as a member of Parliament for one term under Prime Minister Pierre Elliott Trudeau; and the general crazy busyness of family life. Despite all the happy times, Joyce hasn't been without sadness. When she was 25, her and Hu's first child Tommy died from polio, and later, in 1986, Hu died from a massive coronary, shocking Joyce with its abruptness. But Joyce has enjoyed these last few years; her always constant love of cooking, family and friends has brought her to the new career of writing.

Joyce is thrilled to publish her first book and hopes that her memoirs, essays and poems give readers the knowledge that life does continue, even happily, after a profound loss. In her words, "my wish is that as you read my book, you will reflect on your past, how it has shaped your life and the lives of those around you. Then you will decide, if you haven't already, to make your life warmly satisfying."